TheTithe That Binds

Rory O Moore

Faithful Publishing
Buford Georgia

faithfulpublishing.com

Published by
Faithful Publishing
PO Box 345
Buford, Georgia 30515
888-860-5394
faithfulpublishing.com

ISBN: 0-9759941-5-8

Bible verses quoted are from the King James text and/or the Numeric English New Testament Translation by Dr. Ivan Panin

All references to Strong's Exhaustive Concordance of the Bible by James Strong, is taken from the 1980 Edition by Abington Press

Managing Editor: April S Fields
Copy Editor: Dwora Jawer
Cover: April S Fields

I dedicate this book to the Lord God and our Saviour Jesus Christ Who never fails to show me the way when I spend the time and effort to be taught of God according to the Scripture.

Foreword

- *Where is tithing found in the New Testament?*
- *Must the New Testament Church keep the Law of Moses?*
- *Is the local church now the storehouse?*
- *Why do churches need so much money?*
- *Where did the New Testament believers send their gifts?*
- *Is the New Testament ministry to live from tithes?*

These questions and more find their answers in Scripture and the answers may surprise you. If you read this book carefully and without prejudice, you will find many thoughtful and challenging questions and points worth considering. This is not written as a criticism of the Church, God knows we are all fallible, but began as a personal study regarding the ten percent tithe and the Church.

Under inspiration, my wife and I recognized the hand of God as we began to write. At key times, God spoke a Scripture reference for me to look up in the Bible, and then would open my understanding of how it did, or did not, fit the Church. As God continued to add to our understanding, and the anointing of 1 John 2:27 taught us, line upon line unfolded from Scripture until the point came where we realized this is an important message to the Church.

As young Christians, then leaders, elders, and supportive pillars in the Church body, we have dutifully practiced tithing and giving. Our Christian odyssey took us through four churches, and under ten different pastoral ministries. It was a casual remark from a former pastor's wife in regard to tithing becoming "a chore" that initiated our searching out the matter for ourselves from the Bible, and the results were, frankly, startling.

It is said the Bible speaks more to our financial stewardship than many other subjects. If that statement is true, then this is an important work. We hope you do not take our word or conclusions for yourself, but that you, too, will prayerfully search the Scriptures and let God establish what is truth in your heart. We are to obey God rather then man and God is no respecter of persons. If man is wrong and God reveals the error, we are to repent and walk in greater light. The fact that God sends revelation to the body of Christ and calls some to separate from their traditions is a well-established pattern in the historical life of the Body of Christ. Pointing out error in a church's teaching or doctrine is not sowing discord; Paul the apostle publicly corrected or exposed error at least ten times in Scripture, even naming names. Peace at any price is a formula for disaster, and error brings discord. Historically, the establishment church has always resisted fresh revelation, whether from the prophets, Jesus, Luther, or the early Pentecostals, and now this. Jesus Himself came and called out a remnant from the apostate church of Israel with its fragmented sectarianism and leaven.

This book is dedicated to those who want to hear and follow the voice of the Great Shepherd, Jesus Christ.

We wish to thank those who offered suggestions: my wife Linda, Bob Aicardi, and our publisher April Fields.

We are also thankful to those who expressed disagreement. The objections and arguments you gave always motivated us to pray and study the contrary view. In the end, these arguments helped to more firmly establish from Scripture the conclusions of this book.

To our friends in the ministry, pastors, evangelists, and lay leaders, we have no personal axe to grind, we have no ill-will or grudge toward anyone, nor are we singling out any church or ministry in particular. This work is precept-driven in principle and the church world in scope. We pray you God's blessing and the knowledge of His will.

To our former pastor and his wife, Doug and Susan Young, we thank you for your prayers and graciousness. May you understand the joy and fulfillment we have found in Christ. "*The Lord is my shepherd, I shall not want.*"

Some Biblical History

The custom of tithing was established and practiced in the Old Testament and is not arguable. It was a direct, expressed command found within the laws and ordinances of God. Even before the Law that was given to Moses, the great Patriarch Abraham tithed to Melchizedek. His grandson Jacob also pledged a tithe. In the Law of God, (the Torah, the first five books of the Bible), the tithe and other commands, laws, and ordinances were codified in the body of God's Law, which governed ancient Israel and was given to them directly from Jehovah God. The word *tithe* means *tenth*, which is ten percent.

Table of Contents

Chapter 1

Before the Law,
Abraham the Patriarch of Israel and the Church

The connecting thread of the life of Abraham winds through Genesis, the Gospels, Galatians, Hebrews, and many other books in the Bible. He is presented as a role model to those who live a Godly life by faith.

The first direct reference of a tithe is the Genesis example of Abraham tithing to the priest Melchizedek after the recovery of property, persons, and the spoil of battle from an unsavory alliance of heathen bandits. At face value, this passage has been used to illustrate how we are to tithe as did Abraham. Because of the circumstances and a joyous recovery of persons and property near and dear to him, Abraham was so filled with thankfulness and rejoicing for what God had done that he purposed in his heart to give a tenth of the spoils to Melchizedek. Regarding this tithe, we note it was Abraham, not Melchizedek, who initiated a gift of a tenth of the spoil of battle.

Reading between the lines we see that he offered a tithe from a very grateful heart for what God had done for him in the battle. Further study reveals that God had previously promised covenant blessing and protection for Abraham and his seed. Genesis 13:1-2 tells us that, *"Abraham was very rich in cattle, gold, and silver,"* **long before he tithed**, before the fight with the heathen kings! Furthermore, though many assume he did, there is no on-going Biblical record of a continued tithe from Abraham. For many years before he tithed, the Bible speaks of his great faith and wealth and that the blessing of God was with him.

Abraham had a promised son, Isaac, who walked in his father's spiritual footsteps and also inherited the great wealth of Abraham. There is simply no Biblical record of Isaac tithing to anyone, yet there is a record of his great temporal blessings.

Isaac had two sons, Esau and Jacob. Jacob was the spiritual, chosen son, whom God would honor with the blessings of Abraham and the birthright of the firstborn. In regard to tithing in Genesis 28:22, Jacob's tithe reveals again it was Jacob who initiated a tithe promise to God in response to his fear of Esau and hope for God's deliverance. He pledged a tithe but it is not stated who received the tithe. We are not told how he carried out his pledge and we cannot add to Scripture in determining to whom or where it went.

About 400 years after Jacob, came Moses, the deliverer of God's people. It was Moses who received the commandments and ordinances from God (the first five books of the Bible) which codified man's approach to God under the Law of God. This is called the Old Testament, God's expressed will to a covenant people, and was affirmed by the prophets until a New Testament covenant was brought forth to the Christian church by Jesus Christ the Messiah.

In regard to tithing, we have examples of Abraham, Jacob, commands from the Law, prophets such as Malachi, the rich young ruler along with the Pharisees interviewed by Jesus, and the passage in Hebrews 7:4-9, which recounts the Abrahamic and Levitical tithes as examples of passages where a tithe is mentioned either before or as under the Law of Moses.

If we follow the thread of Abraham's life experience with God from Genesis, the four Gospels, Romans and Galatians, through to Hebrews, we find mention, only once, of him tithing to Melchizedek,(recognized as a theophany, i.e., a visitation of Christ before His incarnation) and that is in Hebrews.

In addition to tithing, there are important parallel themes associated with Abraham's life mentioned in the New Testament: faith, circumcision, blood sacrifice, the Laws given at Sinai, and the promises of God's great blessing.

Yes, Abraham Tithed Before the Law of Moses, AND He Also...

In his faith works, Abraham was a circumciser as well as a tither. Galatians and Hebrews both include passages about the faith of Abraham and the promises of God to him and his seed. If we only read the verses that say "Abraham paid tithes" before the Law, it seems correct to teach tithing to the Church. If types and shadows mean anything, paying a faith tithe to Melchizedek as Christ pre-incarnate (Melchizedek being the type or shadow, Christ the substance) may not hold the road to Jesus' ministry because Jesus received no tithes! Christ, and Paul after Him, gave the Gospel without charge. Christ gave freely, yet His needs were provided for. If anyone deserved tithes, it was Jesus Christ, yet He never received the tithe from His followers.

But wait! There is also another ***everlasting covenant*** for Abraham and his seed, and that is the covenant of circumcision. Genesis 17:7-14 says, "*And I will establish my covenant between me and thee and thy seed after thee in their generations for an everlasting covenant, to be a God unto thee, and to thy seed after thee. (8) And I will give unto thee, and to thy seed after thee, the land wherein thou art a stranger, all the land of Canaan, for an everlasting possession; and I will be their God. (9) And God said unto Abraham, **Thou shalt keep my covenant** therefore, thou, **and thy seed after thee** in their generations. (10) This [is] my*

covenant, which ye shall keep, between me and you and thy seed after thee; *Every man child among you shall be circumcised. (11) And ye shall circumcise the flesh of your foreskin; and it shall be a token of the covenant betwixt me and you. (12) And he that is eight days old shall be circumcised among you, every man child in your generations, he that is born in the house, or bought with money of any stranger; which [is] not of thy seed. (13) He that is born in thy house, and he that is bought with thy money,* **must needs be** *circumcised: and my covenant shall be in your* **flesh for an everlasting covenant**. *(14) And the uncircumcised man child whose flesh of his foreskin is not circumcised, that soul shall be cut off from his people; he hath broken my covenant."*

This **tithing-before-the-Law** scenario further unravels when you consider the passage in Matthew 19:4-10, where Jesus discussed divorce and remarriage **before the Law**. *"And he answered and said unto them, Have ye not read, that he which made [them] at the beginning made them male and female, (5) And said, For this cause shall a man leave father and mother, and shall cleave to his wife: and they twain shall be one flesh? (6) Wherefore they are no more twain, but one flesh. What therefore God hath joined together, let not man put asunder. (7) They say unto him, Why did Moses then command to give a writing of divorcement, and to put her away? (8) He saith unto them, Moses because of the hardness of your hearts suffered you to put away your wives: but* **from the beginning it was not so** *(author's note: that is, no divorce before the Law), (9) And I say unto you, Whosoever shall put away his wife, except [it be] for fornication, and shall marry another, committeth adultery: and whoso marrieth her which is put away doth commit adultery. (10) His disciples say unto him, If the case of the man be so with [his] wife, it is not good to marry."*

11

In order to justify tithing before the Law and be consistent, you must now deal with the *"everlasting covenant of circumcision"* and those who are divorced. If divorce was not allowed before the Law, the church must consider those who have remarried to be adulterers and all males must be circumcised!

The modern Church has selected only one of Abraham's works and not the other, **as circumcision was also before the Law**. We are taught that we are the children of Abraham, yet God did not direct Abraham to tithe, but God **commanded** him regarding **circumcision**. A careful reading of the passage tells us that Abraham initiated the gift of his tithe. Three works that Abraham observed were all rolled forward and confirmed into the Law. There can be no denial of this. Why, then, has only tithing been enjoined as a practice from **before the Law**? Who determined we could be so selective when it comes to the practices of faith from **before the Law**?

Galatians 3 plainly states that the covenant came before the Law. *(16)* **"Now to Abraham and his seed were the promises made...** *(17) And this I say, [that]* **the covenant, that was confirmed before** *of God in Christ,* **the law, which was four hundred and thirty years after."** *Hebrews 7 bears witness to the precept of the incorporation of tithing and circumcision embodied and codified in the Old Testament Law. (4) "Now consider how great this man [was] unto whom even* **the patriarch Abraham gave the tenth of the spoils. (5) And verily they that are of the sons of Levi, who receive the office of the priesthood, have a commandment to take tithes of the people <u>according to the law</u>,** *that is, of their brethren,* **<u>though they come out of the loins of Abraham</u>."**

If we claim tithing was before the Law and is applicable to the Church, why is Malachi 3:10 quoted?

This early mosaic from the Santa Maria Maggorie Basillica in Rome depicts the biblical account of Abraham's tithe to the high priest Melchizedek, before the Law was given to Moses.

Genesis 14:18-20 *And Melchizedek king of Salem brought forth bread and wine...And he blessed him, and said, Blessed be Abram... And blessed be the most high God, which hath delivered thine enemies into thy hand. And he gave him tithes of all.*

Chapter 2

Let's Talk Malachi

In Malachi 3:8-11 we find, "*Will a man rob God? Yet __ye have robbed me__. But ye say, Wherein have we robbed thee? In tithes and offerings. (9) Ye [are] cursed with a curse: for ye have robbed me, [even] this whole nation. (10) Bring ye __all the tithes__ into __the storehouse__, that there may be meat in mine house, and prove me now herewith, saith the LORD of hosts, if I will not open you the windows of heaven, and pour you out a blessing, that [there shall] not [be room] enough [to receive it]. (11) __And I will rebuke the devourer for your sakes__, and he shall not destroy the fruits of your ground; neither shall your vine cast her fruit before the time in the field, saith the __LORD__ of hosts.*"

Around 10:30 a.m. to 11:15 a.m. every Sunday morning, someone, somewhere, in each of thousands of churches, reads this passage as they prepare to take the offering. There it is, folks, right there in our faces for all those guilty God-robbers! "It's time to stop robbing God; fork it over to us so God can bless you and rebuke the devourer." Countless guilt-ridden church attendees look down and hide their eyes, squirm nervously in their pews, and think about the times they fudged on paying God ten percent on their business or paycheck, or maybe they just plain forgot something and now God is going to say, "**Gotcha!**" A few tears of guilt are shed, "Oh, God, so that's why my dog died, I got fired, and our son broke his arm! Forgive me!" Some think of their past robbery of the tithe and think they will never be forgiven for the years of this crime they can never repay.

Others sit back smugly, feeling free because they put in the whole paycheck tithe and look around the room smiling, adding to the torment of the guilty. They give their halos a little rub to make them shine a bit brighter, knowing all is well.

On occasion, the leader even goes in front with an Amway dry-erase board and easel (from the days before Power-Point) to carefully explain and diagram what constitutes ten percent. "You make $1,000 and you pay ten percent tithe = $100, and that's **before deductions**," it is emphatically emphasized. "That is $1 for every $10, so if you make $50, your tithe is $5," he writes on the board for those who struggle with math. And, "Oh, yes, birthday and Christmas money, too," he responds to a question. Squirm, squirm for the majority. The leader smiles benignly; he speaks fluent Malachi. This scene we observed countless times. One leader also calculated the interest God required if you were behind in your tithes!

Some churches actually make members show their pay stubs and tax returns to establish the correct amount of their tithes due and charge interest if members fall behind! Many churches keep detailed records of member giving and woe to folks if they do not pay their tithes. A knock on the door finds an unannounced group of church elders and the pastor on their doorstep some evening, all there to correct the wayward and possibly rebellious church member. This happens more often than you would like to imagine.

Now, back to Malachi. What the man up there with the Bible, and maybe the easel, missed, is right there in Malachi. The last time I sat in the church, a lay minister was speaking (the same man was usually either sick or injured and could not keep regular work in spite of the blessing of being a tither). He was quoting from the above verses in Malachi as he admonished the faithful to "pay your tithes." As he spoke, my eyes wandered over to Malachi 3:7 to the word, *ordinances*. "Huh?" I thought, "What ordinances?" Hmmm, it seemed I was going to need a Bible, concordance, and dictionary to learn this *Malachi-speak*.

So I read in Hebrews about those Levi's guys getting ordered to take tithes from the folks. Well, fancy that, they had my favorite pants back there in old Israel and they probably used that tithe money to start up a jeans company!

And I wondered if Malachi's *ordinances* were the same as the ones Moses gave to Israel and that were mentioned in many other places throughout Scripture. We may have people not only robbing God here, but they might be doing a lot of other bad stuff. So maybe we ought to take a closer peek at some of those ordinances.

I found 2 Chronicles 33:8, "... *so that they will take heed to do all that I have commanded them, **according to the whole law and the statutes and the ordinances by the hand of Moses**.*" Yup, they sure had some ordinances back there from Moses alright, lots of them! Six hundred and thirteen of them, they say.

Then it happened, to borrow a word from Gomer Pyle of the old Andy Griffith Show, "Shazzam!" (properly pronounced with a Carolina accent) Up popped Ephesians 2:15, "***Having abolished in his flesh the enmity, [even] the law of commandments [contained] in ordinances.***" Right there in the New Testament it says, "***abolished***."

Meanwhile, back at the church, an ill-wind is blowing; discord among the tithing brethren begins to rumble. A few begin to pray about this point of Law no one has ever challenged or noticed. Tithes? Ordinances? Robbing God? Precious few

16

will seriously study and ask God about it, most find it is easier to toe the party line than ask questions that won't be answered.

Something is obviously wrong with the person asking questions contrary to church teaching! It sounds like "sowing discord," Bubba's rebellion, or "murmuring," after all, how could the church and my pastor possibly be wrong?

As it turned out, I found that in order to speak and understand Malachi, one had to be a Hebrew, and preferably a lawyer. No wonder it was a chore to learn Malachi, I was a non-Jewish gentile and lawyers were people I always had to hire!

Then, as I searched the concordance for *tithe*, I found Paul, Peter, and John, those King James guys and other translators, just plain forgot to put that tithe *in any of the Church epistles or to the preachers*! Can you imagine that?

"Don't worry; Abe tithed before the Law and anyway, since God owns it all, let's just go ahead and use ole Abe as an example for a place to start giving," says the ordained-Bible-college-degree-toting-fella packing Biblical heat. "You want to keep your place in the church, now, right? So giving me your tithe is an act of worship, understand?"

Rumble, rumble. Hmmm, apparently ole Abe in the Good Book may have only tithed one time! I just could not find another time where he blessed someone with another tithe or two. Hey, mister pastor, we decided to follow Abe's tithe, we are going to do it one time, just like ole Abe! "Honey, go ahead and write out that tithe check to Melchizedek!"

But It's Okay, We're Under Grace

We say we are under grace, not Law, so why do we quote Malachi and Leviticus regarding tithing and the laws and ordinances given to Old Testament Israel?

The phrase, *all the tithes,* in Malachi, used to extract ten percent of your gross paycheck, had far more to do with agricultural livestock and produce. And *all* the tithes not only meant the Israelites first fruits, but it meant the numerous other *tenths* they were to pay. Included with tithes were mandated offerings, vows, sacrifices, burnt offerings, and an every third year tithe on top of the rest.

Just check out Deuteronomy 12:11, "*Then there shall be a place which the LORD your God shall choose to cause his name to dwell there; thither shall ye bring all that I command you; your <u>burnt offerings</u>, and your sacrifices, **your tithes**, and the <u>heave offering</u> of your hand, and all <u>your choice vows</u> which ye vow unto the LORD.*" Also look at Nehemiah 13:5, "*And he had prepared for him a great chamber, where aforetime they laid the meat offerings, the frankincense, and the vessels, **and the tithes** of the corn, the new wine, and the oil, which was **commanded [to be given] to <u>the Levites</u>, and <u>the singers</u>, and porters; and the offerings of the priests.*"

Whoops! Who got the tithe back then?

And don't forget another tithe Malachi reminded them of from Numbers 18:26, "*When ye take of the children of Israel the <u>**tithe**</u> which I have given you from them for your inheritance, then ye shall offer up a heave-offering of it for Jehovah, a <u>**tithe**</u> of the <u>**tithe**</u>.*"

Then there is the twenty percent added redemption of the tithing fees from Leviticus 27:31, "*And if a man will redeem aught of his **tithe**, he shall add unto it the fifth part thereof.*" That's right, folks, if you want to keep tithing correctly, you better kick in an additional twenty percent for the redemption of any tithes overlooked. (Refer to the chapter, "So You Think You Are A Tither?")

In Deuteronomy 26:12 is the every third year tithe on the increase above the first fruits tithe. Note to whom it went and that it was a tithe they could eat (no mention of money there). *"When thou hast made an end of tithing **all the tithes** of thine increase the third year, [which] is the year of tithing, and hast given [it] unto the <u>Levite</u>, the <u>stranger</u>, the <u>fatherless</u>, and the <u>widow</u>, that they may eat within thy gates, and be filled."*

Here's another little tithe in Leviticus 5:11; this one was for sin. *"But if he be not able to bring two turtledoves, or two young pigeons, then **<u>he that sinned</u>** shall bring for his **<u>offering the tenth part of an ephah of fine flour</u>** for a sin offering."* There are actually other smaller tithes such as these, so are you sure you want to keep the law of the Old Testament tithe? Yes, if you are going to bring all the tithes into the storehouse, then you have other tithes to pay.

You see, somewhere, someone figured out they would zero in on the ten percent tithe, focus on money, and apply it to the Church, then religion grabbed it and ran with it. Tradition institutionalized it and the average Christian obeyed their leadership and paid, even though it was never God's command to the Church, as giving is.

The truth is, every time Malachi 3 is quoted to the Church about tithing, we are guilty of reviving the Law, which, thank God, has been fullfilled by Christ.

As touching the Law and tithing, the same is true regarding the passage where Jesus spoke to the rich young ruler, a tither, whom Jesus asked, "Have you kept the commandments?" To this question, the rich young ruler replied in Luke 8:12, "I fast twice in the week, I give *tithes* of all that I possess." Other passages, such as those describing the religious Pharisees who tithed, and those in Hebrews 7 and 8, speak of the significance of the pre-Christ priesthood. They all were written or spoken to those under, or familiar with, Old Testament law and covenant. Concerning the tithe, when Jesus told the Pharisees, "*this ought ye have done*," He affirmed the commandments, as He taught others to keep the commandments.

And Paul, in addressing Hebrew Christians, spoke to those familiar with the Law and Commandments. In Hebrews 7, he writes of tithing from before the Law, beginning with Abraham, and continuing through the tithe going to the Levites, as under the Law.

In Galatians 3, the apostolic writer said the same thing in regard to the Abrahamic covenants and promises being confirmed (verse 17) by the law, as quoted previously. He never told the Galatians to emulate Abraham in tithing, although he spoke of Abraham's faith. The Law confirmed tithing, circumcision, blood sacrifice, Sabbath-keeping, religious and human government as the agreement between ancient Israel and God.

Remember, Abraham was more a circumciser and animal sacrificer than he was a tither, and the Old Testament Law confirmed these practices in the *seed of Abraham*. May we ask, when the writer of Hebrews 8 spoke of Abraham tithing, did he say anything in the passage that indicated we are to do likewise? Again, to tell the Church to pay tithes as in Abraham's example, you must (under penalty of Biblical curse) add to the Scripture because it is not in the passage!

It is also very evident the early Church wrestled with these issues of the Old Testament Law and grace. The period of the writing of New Testament Scripture was a transition period in which practices of the Old Covenant and the New were reconciled and resolved. This was illustrated at the Council of Jerusalem in Acts 15. The books of Galatians, Colossians, Ephesians, and various chapters of Romans speak to Church issues such as Sabbath observance, circumcision, feasts, fellowship between Jews and Gentiles and other points. Until the final destruction of the Jerusalem temple in 70 A.D., Levites were probably still receiving tithes as indicated in Hebrews 7:5. *"And verily they that are of the sons of Levi, who receive the office of the priesthood, have a commandment to take tithes of their brethren* (author's note: their Hebrew brethren) *according to the law."* However, in none of the aforementioned Church epistles was tithing specified or directed as an observance to keep. In fact, Acts 21:23 speaks directly to the issue of the Mosaic Law and gentile believers. *"Do therefore this that we say to thee: We have four men which have a vow on them; (24) Them take, and purify thyself with them, and be at charges with them, that they may shave [their] heads: and all may know that those things, whereof they were informed concerning thee, are nothing; but [that] thou thyself also walkest orderly, and keepest the law. (25)* ___As touching the Gentiles which believe, we have written [and] concluded that they observe no such thing___, *save only that they keep themselves from [things] offered to idols, and from blood, and from strangled, and from fornication."*

So you see, while the Old Testament temple stood, the Jewish majority were observing the Law of Moses, including many Hebrew Christians. However, when God used the Roman Empire to destroy the Israel nation and the temple, there was a finality which made those observances impossible to keep anymore. (John 1:17) ***"For the law was given by Moses, but grace and truth came by Jesus Christ."***

Chapter 3

The Storehouse or the Institution in the New Testament?

Where is the New Testament storehouse? Is it the church organization and building on the corner, or is the actual New Testament temple the Body of Christ? We quote 1 Corinthians 3:9 and 16. *"For we are laborers together with God: ye are God's husbandry, [ye are] God's building. (16) Know ye not **that ye are the temple of God**, and [that] the Spirit of God dwelleth in you?"*

This begs the question, to which temple were we tithing, the typical 501c3 corporate, legal institution with a building facility most Christians are members of, or the temple of His body of believers? Consider the chicken dinners, special offerings, auctions, raffles, tithes, bake sales, and all the fundraising done for the building, property, and maintenance of almost every organization that calls itself a *church* versus the Biblical model, where giving went directly to the needy, widows, and poor. Of course, the Church met in houses in those days and most ministers worked and lived a simpler lifestyle. The apostles were given over to prayer and study of the Scripture, God providing for them in an obviously simple lifestyle. Remember Peter's words in Acts as met a lame man, *"**silver and gold have I none**; but such as I have give I thee: In the name of Jesus Christ of Nazareth, rise up and walk*!" By today's standard and thinking, Peter could never reach his large city without a building, advertising, television, etc.

And from where does the practical support for apostles, pastors, teachers, evangelists, and prophets come? In one example, those whom Jesus sent went out with these instructions in Mark 6:8, "*and he charged them that they should take nothing for [their] journey, save a staff only; no bread, no wallet, no money in their purse.*" Here we see the Lord's messengers sent with a promise of divine provision. Could it be that those truly sent by God will receive their provision without tithes and church salaries, merely by God speaking to others who are led of God to supply them? Could this be the case and example of the many ministers of God, both Old and New Testament, where they were provided for in their full-time, working-for-God ministry?

It is mainly pastors who take tithes from the people, but the Bible speaks of the Church having a **five-fold ministry** (apostles, prophets, evangelists, teachers, pastors) and the Biblical record never speaks of New Testament church ministries receiving tithes! Could it be those true Gospel ministers lived by faith, or worked, and God provided for them without salaries and tithes? Did Jesus receive tithes? Did Paul instruct Timothy, Phillip, or Titus to take tithes? Scripture verse, please?

(1 Tim. 5:17) "*Let the elders* (author's note: elders are ALL of church overseers, not just the pastor) *that rule* (author's note: rule means to feed, tend as a shepherd) *well be counted worthy of double honor, especially they who labor in the word and doctrine. (18) For the scripture says, thou shalt not muzzle the ox that treadeth out the corn. And, the laborer is worthy of his reward.*" There is no mention of tithe, and no mention of pastor, either. It says *elders* (plural) and, the word *reward* does not translate into *tithe*.

2 Corinthians 11:8 says that Paul took *wages* (Strong's definition: rations, stipend, or pay) from churches in order to serve the Corinthians. The implication is that several churches

voluntarily funded Paul's ministry with an unnamed amount to support his missions work; again, there is not a single reference to him receiving their tithe. He also wrote, *"they that preach the gospel should live of the gospel"* (he did not mention a tithe.) If Paul was as concerned as our modern church institution about the blessing of God upon the Corinthians, why didn't he quote Malachi to them and tell them about the blessing of tithing, or encourage them to imitate Abraham's tithe? **Neither the Apostle Paul nor any other New Testament writer even once prescribed tithing to any church or saint**. In fact, Paul said in 1 Corinthians 9:18, *"**When I preach the gospel, I make the gospel of Christ without charge**."* The word *charge* means *expense* according to Strong's.

Note this passage from 2 Thessalonians 3:7-9, *"...we were not idle when we were with you, we did not eat anyone's bread without paying, **but with toil and labor we worked night and day**, that we **might not burden any of you**. It was not because we have not that right, but to give you in that conduct an example to imitate."* In this case, Paul worked to set an example for the whole Church, including the pastors, prophets, and teachers so as not to burden the churches he ministered in, unlike the many high-priced evangelists and ministers who expect a generous offering (i.e., wage) for a weekend revival or Sunday service.

For example, Christian writer Tim LaHaye charges $18,000 for a single speaking engagement (according to his website), typical of many big names in the Christian culture. So, of course, this *religious system* around us easily becomes a snare to those called of God, turning them into hirelings.

Paul worked while in Ephesus. He said so in Acts 18:3. *"And because he was of the same craft, he abode with them, and wrought (worked): for by their occupation they were tentmakers."*

24

Paul worked while in Ephesus as noted in Acts 20:34. "*Yea, ye yourselves know, that these hands have ministered unto my necessities, and to them that were with me. (35) I have showed you all things, how that **so laboring ye ought to support the weak**.*"

Paul said he did so for THREE YEARS in vs. 31. That's right: no tithes, no gimmee sermons, no requests for their support! Remember, Paul was addressing the ELDERS and OVERSEERS (Acts 20: 17 And from Miletus he sent to Ephesus, and called the <u>elders of the church</u>.

Paul on his third ministry trip to Corinth, wrote in 2 Corinthians 12:14, "*Behold, the third time I am ready to come to you; and I will not be burdensome to you: for I <u>seek not yours</u> but you: for the children ought not to lay up for the parents, but the parents for the children. (15) And I will very gladly spend and be spent for you; though the more abundantly I love you, the less I be loved. (16) But be it so, <u>I did not burden you</u>: nevertheless, being crafty, I caught you with guile. (17) <u>Did I make a gain of you by any of them whom I sent unto you</u>? (18) I desired Titus, and with [him] I sent a brother. Did Titus make a gain of you? Walked we not in the same spirit? [walked we] not in the same steps?*"

Paul worked in Thessalonica as shown in 2 Thessalonians 3:8. "*Neither did we eat any man's bread for nought; but wrought with labor and travail night and day, that we might not be chargeable to any of you: (9) Not because we have not power, but to make ourselves an ensample unto you to follow us. (10) For even when we were with you, this we commanded you, that if any would not work neither should he eat. (11) For we hear that there are some which walk among you disorderly, working not at all, but are busybodies.*"

Under the Old Testament, the Levites, synagogues, and temple were where the tithes and offerings were expressly commanded to be sent under the Law. The early Church still met in the shadow of the Jerusalem temple while it was yet standing. The pastors, teachers, prophets, evangelists, and apostles either worked or lived strictly by faith and God's provision as the Holy Spirit directed, or from the heartfelt gifts of the saints. Where is any New Testament account of the ministry living from the tithe? The Levite priests received a command under the Old Testament Law to take tithes from the people, as in Hebrews 7:5. "*And verily they that are of the sons of Levi, who receive the office of the priesthood, have a commandment to take tithes of the people according to the law.*" But do any of the New Testament five-fold ministry have a similar command to take tithes of the people? Not in my Bible, nor in yours. The priesthood was changed according to the Scripture and the ministers who teach tithing do not have the Levitical office.

There is 1 Corinthians 9:14, stating, "*the Lord has ordained that they that preach the gospel should live of the gospel,*" but not one mention of tithe. Paul quoted the Old Testament in 1 Timothy 5:18, "*For the scripture saith, thou shalt not muzzle the ox that treadeth out the corn. And, The laborer is worthy of his reward.*" But there is no mention of a tithe. There came a time when Paul no longer labored with his hands and worked for God, and, of course, the Lord still does this. However, He does it His way and not through tithes.

Have you ever heard this one from 1 Corinthians 16:2 at offering time? "*Upon the first [day] of the week let every one of you lay by him in store, as [God] hath prospered him, that there be no gatherings when I come.*" So we dutifully contribute our part as we are expected to do when the plate or bucket is passed. Psst! Hey, we have news for you. The church hijacked that verse, too! We will whisper the verse immediately before that first-day-of-

the-week-give-to-the-church verse they use at the pass-the-plate time: (1 Cor. 16:1) *"Now concerning the collection for the saints, as I have given order to the churches of Galatia, even so do ye."*
Note:
• The *collection* is not a tithe. Does it say tithe? Only if you add to Scripture (under penalty of Biblical curse).
• Does it say for the pastor, ministry, or XYZ organization that calls itself a church? The collection is for the saints.
• Is the word *gatherings* the same as *tithe*? No, the Greek words are totally different.

This apparently was a special offering gathered over the course of a year, and it is not stated that it was to be continued as an unending weekly practice.

Again, no one can honestly teach tithing in this passage without wrestling it into the Scripture. This passage teaches the gathering was for needy saints. The tithe-taking churches are taking from the needy saints.

The church system around us financially manipulates members, taking from the Church to give to the church leadership, programs, and buildings, rather than ministering to the needy within their midst.

Oh, yes, there are some who receive help from their churches but think and compare the crumbs that fall from the church's financial table and what is spent on buildings, seminars, advertising, conventions, concerts, and lavish living. By the way, there is no provision in Scripture for a parsonage (a house provided for a minister by the church). That comes from government and corporate law, not Scripture.

Now, what's that about robbing God we read back in Malachi? We have, through tradition, error, and ignorance, robbed the poor of God's people in our midst by focusing on paying tithes and offerings to a church organization. We have not been taught that Biblical giving, according to the Scripture, is directed toward the needy rather than manmade organizations. We have been, instead, taught to direct our giving toward the local church structure, which is where the overwhelming majority of church funding goes. After all the building, church bills, salaries and utilities are paid, then we can fund a benevolence account, missionary work, and food pantry.

It also has affected our view of people, as we give more respect to those of the middle class and wealth because of their ability to *bless the kingdom*. I say that to our shame and embarrassment, may God forgive us. The Bible clearly calls this *respect of persons*.

(2 Cor. 8:11) "*Moreover, brethren, we do you to wit of the grace of God bestowed on the churches of Macedonia; (2) How that in a great trial of affliction the abundance of their joy and their deep poverty abounded unto the riches of their liberality. (3) For to [their] power, I bear record, yea, and beyond [their] power [they were] willing of themselves; (4) Praying us with much entreaty that we would receive the gift, and [take upon us] the fellowship of the ministering to the saints. (9:9) As it is written, He hath dispersed abroad; he hath given to the poor: his righteousness remaineth for ever.*"

(Rom. 15:26) "*For it hath pleased them of Macedonia and Achaia to make a certain contribution for the poor saints which are at Jerusalem.*"

(Gal. 2:10) "*Only [they would] that we should remember the poor; the same which I also was forward to do.*"

(Psa. 41:1) "*Blessed [is] he that considereth the poor: the LORD will deliver him in time of trouble.*"

Once again, there is a huge gulf between the almost weekly reminders and teaching on the tithe, offering, and give-to-the-church collections with what both Jesus and Paul said to believers in regard to remembering the poor. Next time you go to church, look at the little envelope and all the little choices you can make to fund that organization, and remember what Paul said in Romans 15:26. *"For it hath pleased them of Macedonia and Achaia to make a certain contribution for the poor saints which are at Jerusalem."* And in Proverbs 19:17, *"He that hath pity on the poor lendeth unto the Lord; and that which he hath given will he pay him again."*

If we are walking with God in obedience and hearing His voice, then we are the temple storehouse. As God wants us to minister, He speaks to our hearts to take from what He has given us and minister to whom He directs. That is how Paul was provided for. There is no central building storehouse recorded for Christians to support in the New Testament as the Israelites did in the Old Testament temple.

Another overlooked assumption taken for granted to be the truth is calling a church *the storehouse*. For some it is a shock to realize there is no New Testament verse calling the church building, group, or organization **The Storehouse**.

fp

Chapter 4

When Church Giving Is Not Giving To The Church

Biblical churches met in homes for the most part. There was no overhead, no paid clergy, no staff, no large building, no advertising, no fundraisers, no music department, no drama department, and visiting ministers were able to stay with fellow Christians in their homes. Can you imagine the blessing those early Christians had, to have Paul, Timothy, or Philip stay in their homes? And the wonderful, Godly words of faith the children heard? And to see the miracles, signs and wonders done by God through those powerful Christians? Can you imagine how fast you would walk out of that house church if they sold books, CDs, or raffle tickets when you walked into the entry, or if the hosts asked for money to help pay their household bills when you met every week? If you look in a concordance for the word *house* in the New Testament you may be astounded by what you find relative to Christians gathering. And while you are at it, look up the word *storehouse* in the New Testament for another eyebrow raiser.

Choose which you think might most please God:
• *$1,000 to a poor family to help with food and needs?*
• *$1,000 for new sound equipment, building fund, or budget?*
• *$1,000 to a white-suited, jet-flying TV evangelist?*
• *$1,000 tithe to the Mercedes-driving pastor of a mega-church?*

Which most fits the expressed, written will of God to the Church? Which is most likely to be a blessing to the giver and the receiver? Which do you think most pleases God according to Scripture?

30

As soon as we organize it, name it, build it, incorporate it, and give life to it, the institution of the church cries for funding! And although Christians think they are helping the kingdom and/or the church, they are, for the most part, in reality, supporting a legal institution that is married to the State, and calls itself the XYZ Church.

A mega-church (that promotes tithing) in Houston right now (2005-2006) is spending $70 million dollars to remodel the facility. Source: www.missoulian.com/articles/2004/10/10/religion/religion01.txt

Unfortunately Christians in America have done far more in financially supporting corporate institutions, overhead, and so-called ministry than they have in ministering to the needs of those around them! So, in the New Testament, to whom or what did the collections, gifts, and contributions go? Those questions everyone needs to reread, think about, and then read their Bible to find the correct answers.

Churches will fundraise and goal set for $25,000 on a roof replacement while individual members, single moms, and the elderly barely get by. Is something out of focus here?

As a result of the inequities, there is an uncounted army of Christians who will not set foot in a church building, or who live a cycle of church-hopping, or who now simply reject *churchianity*. The American church model has spawned millions of members and for many, it works, especially new believers who are naïve to the system. But the institutional church has also left millions of believers jaded with Christianity, and our society has lost the respect and honor it once held for Christianity. This is the result after ongoing exposures of financial abuse, fraud, phoniness, and church politics. Yet, many aspire to the ministry and all of the perks of leadership and the system lives on.

And why do churches take up a weekly offering every time they meet? Why, of course, it is to meet the funding requirements of the organization, rather than the need of those to whom the church is called to minister. But for the average Christian it becomes a marriage of the spiritual and corporate worlds, and it destroys the faith of many.

Could this system be the worldwide religious Babylon about which the apostle John wrote in Revelation 17 and 18 that God would judge with fire? Consider that the harlot religious system was well-favored materially and was in bed with the "kings of the earth."

Who recognizes articles of incorporation, God or the State? Does legal incorporation conform churches to God's kingdom or the world? Could the reference to the great harlot in Revelation 17 be to the corporate, institutionalized church organizations we see all around us that are supported by tithes, fundraising, and offerings? These are questions certainly worth pondering. And if you think we have a Christian government and are a Christian nation, it is time to wake up. The Bible calls the kingdoms and governments of this world *beast kingdoms* and they are given to Satan to rule over! Jesus said "*My kingdom is not of this world.*" and in Hebrews 11 agrees: *14 "For they that say such things declare plainly that they seek a country. 15 And truly, if they had been mindful of that country from whence they came out, they might have had opportunity to have returned. 16 But now they desire a better country, that is, an heavenly."*

Corporations are a part of the beast kingdoms (human governments) of the world, and what happens when a group of believers incorporates? The created organization marries through legal agreement the beast kingdom (government), and is subject to its corporate law, rules, and legal codes. Is it fair to ask, if this is so, can we now say we have the *government incorporated church*? Remember, the Church is the *called-out ones*, not the conformed-to-this-world ones.

It appears the Church has indeed added the leaven of human government to itself. This corporate institutional church illustrates what Jesus said in Mark 8:15. "*And he charged them, saying, Take heed, beware of the leaven of the Pharisees, and [of] the leaven of Herod.*" Herod was the head of the government and the religious leaders were in bed with the government who gave them position, authority, and legal backing.

We are reminded of the admonition from 2 Corinthians 6:14. "*Be ye not unequally yoked together with unbelievers: for what fellowship hath righteousness with unrighteousness? And what communion hath light with darkness?*" Isn't incorporation with the IRS an *unequal yoke* for churches? In Bob Jones University v. United States (461 U.S. 574), the U.S. Supreme Court noted the following about the government's intended purpose for the 501c3: The Court asserts that an exempt organization must "demonstrably serve and be in harmony with the public interest," must have a purpose that comports with "the common community conscience," and must not act in a manner "affirmatively at odds with [the] declared position of the whole Government." Taken together, these passages suggest that the primary function of a tax-exempt organization is to act on behalf of the government in carrying out governmentally approved policies.

Churches were added to IRS Code 501c3 in 1954. When a church or denomination accepts the 501c3 status, that church:
- *Waives its freedom of speech*
- *Waives its freedom of religion*
- *Waives its constitutionally guaranteed rights*

- *Is no longer legally free to speak to the vital issues of the day*
- *Must conform with the IRS law or lose its tax-exempt status*
- *Becomes enrolled as a State-church*

The Church is not visible, the kingdom is to be "*within you*" according to Jesus, in a temple "*not made with hands*." The corporate, legal, visible organizations call themselves churches but they are not. That is only a perception. People wishing to become Christians tend to identify God with the visible structures that call themselves churches, and many find a church organization but they fail to find God! Official church membership and attendance is no guarantee you are part of Christ's Body.

The weekly offerings taken up (an oxymoron?) go mainly to support an organizational structure never given in New Testament Scripture. Institutional church pastors must now be advised from specialists in the field of church financial structure, non-profit status, and have unscriptural church boards in order to conform to the law. Ministers in these churches routinely attend legal and accounting seminars to meet the tax code requirements.

It is interesting that in China, the home church movement is the most dynamic and fastest growing part of the Christian Church in the world! They function without legal status, incorporation, Christian accounting firms, flashy evangelists, stadium events, advertising, marketing, CDs, seminars, and institutional hierarchy. When a true Chinese believer thinks of going to church, it is a very different concept from what an American thinks when he decides to attend church. Because of persecution, Chinese believers meet in secret. The Christians in China gather in homes, just as the early Christians did, and they are thriving even though the beast kingdom of the Red Chinese government persecutes them harshly. There is, of course, a licensed, government-sanctioned, institutional church in China meeting in the larger buildings (and which does not preach the true Gospel). It appears the aging wineskin of our accepted church model is splitting at the seams and suffers from an ongoing need of financial infusion.

Where is the storehouse for a Chinese Christian in Red China with no building or corporate structure? (For that matter, where are the Chinese mega-churches?) Who benefits when the organization furnishes a building? God? Needy people in the Kingdom? Yet the building programs, remodeling, and merchandising of American churches is done in the name of the Kingdom of God.

Could it be that the incorporated, institutional Christian church has fallen into a tradition not substantiated in the New Testament and in becoming bonded to the laws of the land through incorporation, the need for church administration, and ongoing support of overhead, has lost the vision of how and what church really is?

Could it be also that we have been feeding the overhead of the institutional church rather than the orphans, poor, and widows, as Paul wrote and as is spoken of in Scripture? Where is the New Testament Scripture for a church board, and can you name a specific Scriptural example of someone holding this office?

Yes, we have some very impressive buildings, property, and assets, but do we dare compare an advertising budget and church furnishing to what actually goes out in ministry to missions, aid, and needs of the Body of Christ? What of the medical needs of those who have no insurance? Again, how many offerings are gathered or fundraising efforts made to support *church needs* such as property purchases, taxes, insurance, office supplies, remodeling the building, electronic gadgetry, wages, entertainment, meals, and clergy lifestyles? How many collections for the poor have you seen?

The cliché we have all heard, "all churches want is your money," unfortunately contains more than a grain of truth. What many don't realize is that no denomination, organization, building, or incorporated group of Christians is The Church. We only perceive those institutions as being The Church, and they do need our money (especially for the building, mortgage, overhead, staff, and leadership, which typically take 96% of what comes into the church coffers). And most ministers, if they are really honest, would admit they believe bigger is better (in terms of the church size that they personally manage).

In other behind-the-scenes examples, we remember staff discussions comparing who had the best "anointing for taking the offering" and "when so-and-so got up we did not get as much." If one person seemed to inspire the people to contribute more, then that person became the regular offering-taker (during collections a speaker was usually exhorting those in the building as to why they should contribute, using Bible verses). Concern for the mortgage, bills, programs, and church furnishings drove most fundraising and offering times. (Thankfully, the mortgage was paid off later in that church to which we belonged.)

Special speakers usually drew visitors and an increase in the size of the collections, which may or may not have gone to the speaker (depending on the discretion of the particular pastor of the church). There would be talk of offering shortfalls or enough coming to pay the speaker a fair and respectable offering for an hour or so of speaking; $1,000 was typical. The church felt it was correct that each speaker received a generous offering, even if taken from the tithe account.

So why does it become necessary, then, to have someone with the best "offering-anointing" speak over the collection? The answer is obvious: in order to fund the operation of the church and pay the speaker, even if it meant paying them an amount far greater than most members earned from their jobs. This is in stark contrast to the Biblical collections that went to help the needy, and the Gospel ministers such as Paul, who said, *"that I make the gospel without charge."* Titus in 2 Corinthians 12:18 followed Paul's example. *"Did Titus make a gain of you? walked we not in the same spirit? [walked we] not in the same steps?"*

Maybe we need to prayerfully look at the Scriptures regarding the walk of the Biblical preachers in regard to preaching for pay in passages such as 1 Corinthians 9:6. *"Or I only and Barnabas, have not we power to forbear working? (7) Who goeth a warfare any time at his own charges? who planteth a vineyard, and eateth not of the fruit thereof? or who feedeth a flock, and eateth not of the milk of the flock? (8) Say I these things as a man? or saith not the law the same also? (9) For it is written in the law of Moses, thou shalt not muzzle the mouth of the ox that treadeth out the corn. Doth God take care for oxen? (10) Or saith he [it] altogether for our sakes? For our sakes, no doubt, [this] is written: that he that ploweth should plow in hope; and that he that thresheth in hope should be partaker of his hope. (11) If we have sown unto you spiritual things, [is it] a great thing if we shall reap your carnal things? (12) If others be partakers of [this] power over you, [are] not we rather? Nevertheless we have not used this power; but suffer all things, lest we should hinder the gospel of Christ."*

In this passage there is a Scriptural provision providing for the ministry (without any mention of tithes or salaries). The difference is that with the current model of the incorporated church, funding overhead has usurped the ministry to those called of God "*to forebear working*."

The man Saul (Paul) thought he did God's service before he was saved, by persecuting Christians. Likewise we also thought we were doing God's service with all the bake auctions, yard sales, peanut brittle sales, chicken dinners, raffles, gift sales, church yard sales, Halloween harvest parties, etc., etc., etc., in funding the incorporated church.

To summarize the key points of this chapter we would like to say The Church is not an organized group of people with a name or denominational label. The Church is the people of God who have been born again into the family of God and are indwelt by His Spirit. Jesus said this in John 2:21 – "*But he spake of the temple of his body.*" And Paul agreed in Eph. 2: 19 "*Now therefore ye are no more strangers and foreigners, but fellowcitizens with the saints, and of the household of God; 20 And are built upon the foundation of the apostles and prophets, Jesus Christ himself being the chief corner stone; 21 In whom all the building fitly framed together groweth unto an holy temple in the Lord: 22 In whom ye also are builded together for an habitation of God through the Spirit.*"

As such, the group on the corner may have a storehouse or food pantry for example, but contrary to common teaching, in the New Testament the church is never referred to as the storehouse. This is simply more *leaven* that sounds good. Christians were never called to fund building projects, pastoral and staff salaries, layers of organizational bureaucracy, mega church operations, and such like. All of those masquerade as the church and most Christians perceive them to be such causing them to not be able to recognize Christ's Body. They also cause Christians to mis-direct their giving away from the Church of Christ's Body and give to the various organizations that call themselves churches. Keep in mind the vast majority of those funds collected simply go to the overhead, staff, and operating costs. No wonder the likes of TBN, Benny Hinn, and Jesse Duplantis will not disclose their financials openly.

These and the many who are like them fit the spiritual profile given in Rev. 18:11 as *"the merchants of the earth"* who make their living in spiritual Babylon, the *"Mother of Harlots"*. They make merchandise of God's people and in one of the few demonstrations of outward anger Jesus dealt with their forerunners in the Holy Temple of His day in Mat. 21:12-13 *"And Jesus went into the temple of God, and cast out all them that sold and bought in the temple, and overthrew the tables of the moneychangers, and the seats of them that sold doves, And said unto them, It is written, My house shall be called the house of prayer; but ye have made it a den of thieves."*

Everything Jesus did was also a parable for us, especially those of us in these last days. The temple is no longer a building it is His Body. So in the Body of Christ we now find an abundance of those who change money from the people into an act of worship (so they say). Never mind in Matthew 6:1-4 Jesus said: 1 1 *"Take heed that ye do not your alms before men, to be seen of them: otherwise ye have no reward of your Father which is in heaven. 2 Therefore when thou doest thine alms, do not sound a trumpet before thee, as the hypocrites do in the synagogues and in the streets, that they may have glory of men. Verily I say unto you, They have their reward. 3 But when thou doest alms, let not thy left hand know what thy right hand doeth."*

39

When the plate, bag, or bucket gets passed from left hand to the person on the right, is it not seen of men and given under somewhat of subtle coercion (necessity), institutional expectation, and even orchestrated manipulation? Friend, when it is seen of men, that is the only reward you will get. You may want to remember what Jesus said about this next the next time they pass the plate in the *synagogue* (a people gathering place) called a church in our day.

And if you would *"beware of men in sheeps clothing"* please give consideration to all the gimmee sermons, pleas for money, and our need to "give to the church" that Jesus warned of when He said His house was called a *den of thieves.* You may want to take note the ones who "sold doves" were a type and figure of those who sit in the chief seats in our churches and sell the promise of the Holy Spirit for salaries and tithes. (The dove being a type of the Holy Spirit as pictured at the baptism of Jesus.)

When Jesus sent his true workers out, He did so telling them in Matthew 10:8 *"Heal the sick, cleanse the lepers, raise the dead, cast out devils: freely ye have received, freely give. 9 Provide neither gold, nor silver, nor brass in your purses, (wallets) 10 Nor scrip for your journey, neither two coats, neither shoes, nor yet staves: for the workman is worthy of his meat."*

This pattern held true for not only the Twelve, the seventy, Paul, Barnabbas, Phillip, Titus, and all those sent out by the Christian church in Acts (there is no scriptural account of any of them taking tithes or salaries), but also is a fulfillment of the promise *"I have never seen the righteous forsaken no his seed go begging for bread."* All of which bears no resemblance to the professional clergy and church world around us who have apostasized from the examples of Jesus and His followers in regard

40

to how they are provided for. To *freely give* the gospel does not leave room for tithes and salaries but the institutional servants expect the sheep to provide for them contrary to the Scripture and truly the modern church has become *a den of robbers* all in the name of Christ.

Remember, all this is done without a single verse supporting tithes and salaries from Christians to the clergy in the New Testament Covenant.

Chapter 5

Where Was That Verse Again?

Is the Covenant of Tithing expressly taught or commanded in the New Testament as written to any Gentile church group? Where in Acts, Romans, Corinthians, Galatians, Ephesians, Philipians, Colossians, Thessalonians, Timothy, Titus, Hebrews, James, John, Peter, Jude, or Revelation is tithing specifically instructed for Christians to do?

Here is a blank space for you to write in the verses: _. (The line is real short for good reason.)

Remember, to establish Biblical teaching we must have at least two or three witnesses from a *rightly divided* Scripture. May we ask for the New Testament church tithing witnesses to present themselves from Scripture? *"In the mouth of two or three witnesses let every word be established,"* directly quotes Jesus Christ. Paul was a powerful witness, as were John, James, Luke, Matthew, and Mark. Do any of those men bring witness to instruct Christians to tithe?

A prime location to look for a command, ordinance, or exhortation to tithe would have been in Acts 15 at the great Council in Jerusalem, where Christian church practices were debated concerning Gentile Christians. In the summary of things for Gentiles to abstain from and the things for them to put into practice, tithing is not mentioned, although it was a perfect time to include a reminder of Malachi 3:10.

In Paul's instructions to Timothy, and in the epistles from James, John, and Peter, *tithe*, *tithing*, or *tenth* is never referred to.

In the passage from 1 Corinthians in regard to a collection of *gatherings* (contributions) on the first of the week, as God has prospered, there is no mention of the word *tithe*. The collection was for *saints*, it was from *gatherings* (contributions), again, a perfect place to insert the word *tithe*, if that is what Paul expected. The collection was not for clergy support or a building, it was for ministry to needy Christians!

In 1 Timothy 4:11, Paul gave Timothy many things to teach the people, saying, *"These things command and teach,"* but there was no mention of a tithe. To the Corinthians, he wrote, (1 Cor. 14:37) *"If any man think himself to be a prophet, or spiritual, let him acknowledge that the things that I write unto you are the commandments of the Lord,"* but, again, he made no mention of a tithe. If Paul did not tell any of his churches to tithe, then who are we to do so?

Repeatedly we have promises such as, *"God loveth a cheerful giver,"* or, *"he that soweth sparingly shall reap also sparingly."* These are all great places in Scripture to remind believers of Malachi and the holy tithe, as the modern church does. In practice, we teach, *"he that tithes sparingly shall reap also sparingly,"* and, *"God loveth a cheerful tither,"* or, *"tithe and it shall be given unto you, pressed down, shaken together, running over shall men give into your bosom."*

And the way Malachi 3:10 is repeated in many churches, you would think the apostles would have quoted it in every church epistle! Many Old Testament Scriptures are quoted throughout the New Testament, but not Malachi 3:10. What a terrible omission by the New Testament writers, especially in the epistles to the churches!

The irony here is that many of the churches that teach and promote tithing don't have full, open disclosure and accountability of church finances. If your church promotes tithing you have the right to demand your pastor's tithe statement and the church tithe too. That, indeed, is the flip-side of the coin for Malachi. But it is a meaningless point because 2 Corinthians 3:14 says, "*the old testament which was done away in Christ*," and Hebrews 7:12 says, "*there is of necessity a change in the law*," continuing with 7:19, "*For the law made nothing perfect*." The passage in Hebrews 7 deals with tithing being before, and then under, the Old Testament Law. That is the context and the writer never went on to reaffirm either the continuation of the Law or tithing! On the contrary, he reaffirms the end of the Law, and tithing was a part of the Law.

No matter how we sugarcoat or reason with it, tithing was commanded under the Law and we are copying and pasting it into New Testament church practice without an express command from Scripture. Every time we quote Malachi 3:10 or similar verses to the Church, we are lifting an expressed ordinance given under the Law, of which Christ said, "*it is finished*," and applying it to post-cross Christians. Abraham tithing before the Law does not negate that the tithe was confirmed forward as a command of the Law, and not a single church or saint was given an expressed doctrine to tithe as Abraham.

Conversely, is a failure to tithe ever named as sin in the New Testament? Not in Romans, nor in the list of works of the flesh in Galatians 6; it is not named in 1 Corinthians 6 as something that will keep one out of the kingdom of God, nor is it mentioned in the list of excluded sins in Revelation 21.

In passages of the New Testament where giving is encouraged and expressly written of, is tithe ever mentioned?

Please fill in the verse: _.

(Again, a very short line).

Is failure to tithe or *robbing God in tithes* listed as sin in Romans 1, 1 Corinthians 6:9-12, or in Galatians under works of the flesh? Was tithing encouraged in Acts 15 at the Jerusalem council as one of the things in which the Gentiles ought to continue? This would be an absolutely perfect place to instruct them as we have, if it is so.

Is tithing mentioned in any of the epistles in connection to giving, gathering, gift, offering, stealing, thieves, or robbers?

No, tithing is not in His Word to the Church. There is <u>no Scriptural authority</u> for any pastor, teacher, apostle, or prophet to lay this yoke of burden on Christians. Tithing is never mentioned as a part of a Christian's duty or relationship with God, never. God never said to the churches or Christians He would bless tithing. *"Obey them that have the rule over you"* does not give a preacher authority to go beyond the Scripture. If Paul, James, John, Peter, and Luke never instructed Christians to tithe, the local pastor certainly shouldn't.

(Rom. 16:17) *"Now I beseech you, brethren, mark them that are causing the divisions (author's note: error divides us from God's Word) and occasions of stumbling, **contrary to the doctrine which ye learned: and turn away from them**."* There is no doctrine of tithing given to the Church. And verse (18) *"For they that are such serve not our Lord Christ, but their own belly; and **by their smooth and fair speech they beguile the hearts of the innocent**."* The innocent Christians are taught to believe an error and are thus divided from God's Word.

Jesus warned, *"Woe unto you lawyers! For you took away the key of knowledge: you entered not in yourselves, and them that were entering in you hindered."* We know of many who became guilt-ridden which hindered their faith when they were taken aside and given the teaching on tithing.

Paul warned church leaders when he wrote in Titus 1:10, *"For there are many unruly men* (author's note: unruly men not abiding in Scripture), *vain talkers and deceivers, specially they of the circumcision* (author's note: circumcision law-keepers), *(11) whose mouths must be stopped; men who overthrow whole houses* (author's note: churches), *teaching things which they ought not for filthy lucre's sake"* (author's note: for instance, teaching the lucrative tithe for personal benefit without a single verse that the New Testament ministry was to take tithes. From the dictionary: lucre \LOO-kuhr\, noun: Monetary gain; profit; riches; money; -- often in a bad sense). *(12) One of themselves, a prophet of their own, said, Cretans are always liars, evil beasts, idle* (author's note: non-working) *gluttons. (13) This testimony is true. For which cause reprove them sharply, that they may be sound in the faith."*

Tithing is of the Law, not of faith and the Lord sends a sharp rebuke to them who teach error and thus are not sound in the faith. And remember, Paul admonished the *overseers* to support themselves and *the weak* rather than taking from them.

A current illustration of what Jude wrote is this interview from the Columbus Monthly about Televangelist Rod Parsley :

Parsley tells his people they should believe for millions. He makes no apology for being mercenary:

"Parsley is upfront with his congregation about the church's need for money. 'I just love to talk about money,' he told them. 'I just love to talk about your money. Let me be very clear — I want your money. I deserve it. This church deserves it.'"

Regarding Parsley's personal holdings, the Columbus Monthly magazine further discloses:

"Parsley, his wife, Joni, and their two young children live in a five-bedroom house they have built next to his parents' house on a 21-acre compound in northwest Fairfield County. The compound has an electronic gate at the road to discourage uninvited visitors, and stables and a corral have been built in one corner. Rod Parsley's home is worth $857,090, say records at the Fairfield County recorder's office. His parents' home, also new, is valued at $831,480. Each was built with a $200,000 mortgage taken out in 1990. ... Parsley also owns a $500,000 jet, a seven-passenger Hawker Siddeley 125."
(Source:www.apostasywatch.com/wolves2/page10.html)

And from Brother Parsley's "Breakthrough" website (www.breakthrough.net/faq.asp):

"Tithing-From the Hebrew word maasrah, meaning tenth. A tenth of our gross (firstfruits), not our net increase Genesis 4:3-4, Genesis 14:18-19, Genesis 28:20-22, Deuteronomy 26:2. We bring the tithe to the priest in his office. In the Old Testament, the priest was a man Deuteronomy 26:3-4. In the New Testament, the priest is Jesus Christ Hebrews 7:5-8. Bring your tithe into the storehouse where you receive spiritual food Malachi 3:10. Make your confession of faith when you bring your tithe Deuteronomy 26:3, Deuteronomy 26:5-11. Withholding tithes or offerings. A tithe withheld must be paid with 20% interest added Leviticus 27:31 It tends to poverty Proverbs 11:24. Robbing God Malachi 3:8-9."

Notice that every verse quoted to take tithes from his followers is from the law, except the verse from Hebrews that referenced those who were (past tense) under the law. The reference to Jesus Christ being our high priest is used here to justify Bro. Parsley receiving the tithe. We ask again, where is Scripture for ANY New Testament pastor, apostle, etc., taking your tithe?

Now re-read the chapter on the end of the law and the verses from Jude, along with the definition for *lucre*, right above, and think, dear Brother and Sister. And ask God to show you truth.

Dare we compare Bro. Parsley, Hinn, Joyce Myers, the TBN crowd, and so many other prominent big time ministries to some of the big names of Scripture? Two prominent men who even bore the same name, Saul, bear striking examples of two kinds of spiritual leaders of God's people.

Consider Paul's word to the Corinthians in IICor. 11: 9 "***And when I was present with you***, (he was with them for a year and a half and ministered there just as he did for the three years he was in Ephesus) *and wanted,* **_I was chargeable to no man_***: for that which was lacking to me the brethren which came from Macedonia supplied: and in all things **_I have kept myself from being burdensome unto you_***, and so will I keep myself. 10 As the truth of Christ is in me, no man shall stop me of this boasting in the regions of Achaia. 11 Wherefore? because I love you not? God knoweth. 12 But what I do, that I will do, that I may cut off occasion **_from them which desire occasion_*** (the word *occasion* means opportunity); that wherein they glory, they may be found even as we. 13 For **_such are false apostles, deceitful workers_***, transforming themselves into the apostles of Christ."*

Now let's look at another Saul back in I Sam. 8-9. This was the physically attractive stand-out of his day, literally. Notice what God said about the man the people of God wanted to rule over them, lead them, and protect them:

*"And he said, **_This will be the manner_** of the king that shall **_reign over you_***: **_he will take_** your sons, and **_appoint them unto him_***, for his chariots, and to be **_his horsemen_***; and they shall run before his chariots; and **_he will appoint_** them unto him for*

*captains of thousands, and captains of fifties; and he will set some to plow his ground, and to reap his harvest, and to make his instruments of war, and the instruments of his chariots. And **he will take the tenth of your seed**, and of your vineyards, and **give to his officers**, and to **his servants**. And he will take your men-servants, and your maid-servants, and your **goodliest young men**, and your mules, **and put them to his work**. **He will take the tenth of your flocks: and ye shall be his servants**. And ye shall cry out in that day because of your king whom ye shall have chosen you..."*

The men who took the ministry of *King* over God's people had a certain *manner*. They took from the people to be their own servants in the name of *serving* the king and they would give homage to the man and defend him. They appointed captains over their programs, administration, staff, and hierarchy. These appointed servants assisted the king in taking up the tenths and fruits of the people in order to fund his administration and organization. They would take of the *"goodliest young men"* and put them to work just like the zealous, young new converts who usually jump into church life with zeal and work the program overseen by the pastor who usually has the chief seat in the church. The mules are the burden bearers known as *pillars* and mainstays of the local church organization who support the church with time, finances, and work. They include the secretaries, teachers, program directors, ushers, businessmen, and others.

Let's summarize these two scriptural examples of characteristics of leadership:

King Saul <u>took</u> of the people servants, tenths, young men and maidens, fell into corruption, and had God's people work for his personal kingdom and vision.

49

The Apostle Paul worked while he served, took nothing, gave utterly of himself, had no servants, and was totally sacrificial in serving the Lord. And when Paul no longer physically worked for wages, he was supplied by giving brethren because of the years he spent both working and ministering to the churches. And note those who worked the works of God healed the sick, worked miracles, signs and wonders rather than administrating a building and organization. Paul's work was "*in the power and demonstration of the Spirit*" rather than in Sunday sermons, books, tapes, and programs.

As you continue to read this book, you will come across other examples of the plundering of God's people for the building of personal kingdoms and organizations in the name of Christianity.

If we are going to site Scripture as the foundation for doctrine let us compare other examples of commands.

Below are two lists of the Scriptures from the New Testament:

1. Examples of Christians or churches tithing:

2. Commands to Christians to tithe:

Contrast this with two lists of Scriptures regarding baptism:

1. Examples of Christians baptized:
   Acts 2:41; 8:16; 9:18; 10:48; 19:5
   Romans 6:3
   1 Corinthians 1:13-14
   Galatians 3:27
   Colossians 2:12

2. Commands for Christians to be baptized:
   Matthew 28:19
   Mark 16:16
   Acts 2:38; 10:48; 22:16

Or compare two lists of Christians keeping the Sabbath:

1. Examples of New Testament Christians meeting on or observing the Sabbath:

Acts 13:14; 13:42; 13:44; 17:2

Luke 4:16; 4:31

2. Commands to Christians to keep the Sabbath:

In these three areas of study we easily develop doctrinal conclusions: Christian baptism is given by both example and command. Christian Sabbath-keeping has only limited examples and no New Testament command. Without an expressed command to Christians and the Church, we are not under the Law to observe the Jewish Sabbath.

Christian tithing has no New Testament example either and no command. Yet we teach it as unshakeable truth for the Church, quoting Malachi 3:10 over and over. Compare this with what Paul told the believers regarding giving in 2 Corinthians 9:7. *"Every man according as he purposes in his heart,* (so let him give), *not grudgingly or of necessity, for God loveth a cheerful giver."* But without an expressed Biblical command or law for the Church to tithe, we have only commands and examples from the Old Testament. Read and compare similar precepts, such as baptism, where we read of New Testament believers receiving a direct command to be baptized and examples of baptisms! In Acts 10:48, Peter "commanded them to be baptized, And they that gladly received his word were baptized both men and women." Both commands and examples are given to confirm the doctrine.

With the Sabbath, we have multiple examples where New Testament believers met or kept the Sabbath, but we have no direct New Testament command to keep the Sabbath. We have examples of Paul and others going up to Jerusalem to keep the feasts, but no such direct command. We have both commands and examples to work, to love, to teach, to baptize, and to pray, but never a direct command to tithe. Another example found in Scripture but which we have no command to duplicate is Zacheus giving half his goods to the poor. The early Church sold their goods and gave into the ministry, apparently the majority going to help the poor and widows. These were done as acts of free-will giving, not as a command.

To conclude, in the New Testament Scriptures, we have neither command nor example for the Church to tithe. To enforce the law of the tithe in the New Testament Church is to re-establish the Law, the need to keep *all* of the Law, and also the opening up of Christians to the curse of the Law according to Galatians 3. Jesus warned, "*Beware of the leaven of the Pharisees.*" What was their leaven? The religious leaders required their converts to keep traditions which God never required, going beyond the Scripture. They kept the rules but missed God, just like the churches that enforce tithing cause believers to miss the leading of the Holy Spirit in giving. (Ecc. 1:9) "*The thing that has been is the thing which shall be.*" The day will come when many Christians realize rules and laws in their churches are a form of Godliness that denies the power thereof.

Chapter 6

Holes In Our Bag Or In Our Theology?

Another Old Testament passage we have heard reminding us of our need to be tithers is from Haggai 1:6-9, "*he that earns wages earns wages to put it into a bag with holes*" and "*you looked for much and lo, it became little*," implying God calling for a drought upon the houses of the Christian non-tithers. But the real hole, here again, is in our theology on tithing. The truth is found in Haggai 2:5, the references are once again in the context of the Law, "*According to the word that I covenanted with you when you came out of Egypt.*" What covenant was that? Who was the word for? Do you want the truth?

The commandments of God were for Israel, not the Church. Again we have an Old Testament precept superimposed on the Church. Is the *house of God* in the Old Testament the same as in the New Testament? They had a physical temple in Jerusalem, Scripture teaches the house or temple in the New Testament is the Body of Christ (or those who believe on Him). **Here are two lists of Scriptures referencing tithing/giving:**

1.(tenth, tithe, tithing)	2. (give, giveth, giving, gift, seed, sow, soweth)
	Matthew 10:8; 10:42; 19:4; 20:8
	Luke 6:30, 6:38; 12:33
	Acts 20:35
	Ephesians 4:28
	Colossians 4:1
	1 Thessalonians 5:18
	2 Corinthians 9:7
	Romans 12:8
	Philipians 4:15

A total of fourteen passages contain a direct, expressed exhortation to give. There are two more verses that refer to *seed sown* and *soweth* in 2 Corinthians 9:16 and 9:10 that refer back to giving and do not mention a tithe. Yet the churches that keep the tithing ordinance must lean on the Old Testament because when they look for tithing in the New Testament, they only find references to giving. Or, they do as our old church did, they blend giving with tithing, teaching from Scriptures on giving, adding in tithing in order to receive God's financial blessing.

What about *firstfruits*, which is also mentioned by the tithe proponents as belonging to God and the church? A scan of Strong's Concordance shows not a single reference to first-fruits or firstfruit in reference to either giving or tithing. The mention of firstfruits in the New Testament has everything to do with Christians themselves being firstfruits to God and the evidence of the Holy Spirit. (Jas. 1:18) *"Of his own will begat he us with the word of truth, that we should be a kind of firstfruits of his creatures."* (Rev. 14:4) *"These are they which follow the Lamb whithersoever he goeth. These were redeemed from among men, [being] the firstfruits unto God and to the Lamb."* (Rom. 8:22) *"For we know that the whole creation groaneth and travaileth in pain together until now. (23) And not only [they], but ourselves also, which have the firstfruits of the Spirit, even we ourselves groan within ourselves, waiting for the adoption, [to wit] the redemption of our body."*

Once again, the proponent of tithing loses his argument for teaching the Church that the firstfruits are to be brought in as a tithe. It is typical teaching in tithing churches that in order for you to have and keep a *blessed* 90% of your wages/harvest/increase, you should tithe that first 10% to them in the name of God.

Remember, in the New Testament, God, indeed, owns it all and we are stewards over 100%. In Luke 14:33, Jesus said, "*So therefore whosoever he be of you that renounceth not <u>all that he hath</u>, he cannot be my <u>disciple</u>.*" That does not sound like the tithe-to-prosper message. We should be hearing His voice to receive constant instruction on the management of His 100%, of which we renounced ownership.

This also goes hand-in-hand with the prosperity teachings that encourage Christians to give in order to get. Many pastors would deny they teach tithing as a give-to-get doctrine. Yet, to the average Christian, who does not read the bible, the tithe-to-be-blessed, firstfruits-redemption-of-the-rest-of-your-finances teaching, breeds an expectation of the guarantee of financial rewards. Corruption is subtly sown in the leadership ministry itself as it gives the minister a financial incentive to *grow the kingdom* of his church. After all, "if you are blessed with a raise, then the pastor is blessed with a raise," (an actual quote from the pulpit).

If a tither receives an inheritance, tax refund, or insurance settlement, then the minister also has an expectation to participate in the bounty. He may feel robbed if the tither is not forthcoming with the expected tithe on those blessings because under the tithing rule, it is due to him. We know of one family who tithed on money that they borrowed to finance their home repairs! That same family labored and struggled financially for years, tithing and offering all the while. The financial abuse caused their two children to turn away from God, and the precious firstfruits of their children have been lost to the kingdom of God. No one bothered to show them from Scripture that God never said borrowing was a form of increase and required a tithe.

How can we quote Apostle Paul, who said we are "*dead to the Law*," when tithing is one of the commands of the Law of the Old Covenant, then turn right around and say the New Testament Church does not need to keep the Law? To do that is to kill the Law, then revive it back into the Church. That is "another gospel" upon which Paul pronounced a curse in Galatians 1:7-8. Abraham's faith and covenants pointed ahead to the promises of God, which resulted in the giving of God's expressed Law 420 years later. The promises of God's blessing upon Abraham, which included the Lord's acceptance of his tithe, sacrifices, and obedience in circumcision, were all confirmed in the Law of Moses. Yet, Paul refers to the "*weak and beggarly elements*," and the "*carnal commandment*" of those things contained in the Law, in which tithing is included. You cannot remove the fact that tithing was part of the Law.

Paul wrote in Colossians 2:20, "*Wherefore if ye be dead with Christ from the rudiments of the world, why, as though living in the world, are ye subject to ordinances?*" Verse 23 continues to say that the practices of old Jewish traditions and laws do have an appearance or show of wisdom, humility, and sacrifice, as does tithing. He adds in Colossians 2:14 that Christ performed the "*blotting out the handwriting of ordinances that was against us, which was contrary to us, and took it out of the way, nailing it to his cross.*" Ephesians 2:15 states, "*Having abolished in his flesh the enmity, [even] the law of commandments (author's note: Old Testament tithing laws included) [contained] in ordinances.*" And Galatians 3:10 reminds us, "*For as many as are of the works of the law are under the curse: for it is written, Cursed [is] every one that continueth not in all things which are written in the book of the law to do them.*" Are you performing the works of the Law? If you tithe, you are in bondage to the Law, even if you deny doing

57

the works of the Law. (Gal. 5:1) "*[A]nd be not entangled again with the yoke of bondage.*"

This is *the tithe that binds.*

Another point of the Law that traced back to Abraham is mentioned in Galatians, and that is circumcision. (Gal. 5:3) "*For I testify again to every man that is circumcised, that he is debtor to do the whole law.*" Keeping an Abrahamic covenant rolled forward and confirmed into the Law obligates us to do the whole Law! Tithing was an Abrahamic practice rolled forward and confirmed into the Law, and in so doing, we become debtors to do the whole Law! Remember we heard tithing was before the law. Well, so were circumcision and blood sacrifice! The very next verse states, "*Christ is become of no effect unto you, whosoever of you are justified by the law.*" Tithing was part of the Law. Again, how can we say we are not under the Law, but then turn around and quote Malachi, Haggai, Leviticus, and teach tithing, which was part of the Law?

By now the supporter of tithing is working even harder to justify Christian tithing and he finds Jesus speaking to the Law-keeping Pharisees in Matthew 23:23. "*Woe unto you, scribes and Pharisees, hypocrites! for ye pay tithe of mint and anise and cumin, and have omitted the weightier [matters] of the law, judgment, mercy, and faith: these ought ye to have done, and not to leave the other undone.*"

Please, take a closer look here, friends. In this passage, when Jesus referred to those things which included tithing as matters "*of the law,*" He was speaking to Pharisees, who were Law-observing, Old Testament Jews. Hebrews 8:4 describes them as "*priests that offer gifts according to the law.*"

The New Covenant in Christ is not in effect before the death of the Testator. (Heb. 9:17) "*For a testament [is] of force after men are dead: otherwise it is of no strength at all while the testator liveth."*

Three points emerge showing the error of applying tithing to the Church from these passages:

- *Jesus referred to tithing as pertaining to the Law.*
- *The Pharisee was under the Old Covenant Law.*
- *The New Covenant is not in effect while the testator lives.*

Warning! The next time you hear *"tithing was before the Law"* and the speaker tries to disconnect it from Moses' Law, he is contradicting Jesus, Who included tithing in the matters of the Law.

Once again, the law of tithing collides head-on with the New Testament teaching in Romans 6:14, *"Ye are not under the law, but under grace."* Yet, sadly, an army of Bible-college-educated ordained ministers repeat and compound the error of tithing and fundraising. In effect, they are robbing God's people, and creating their own kingdoms supported by an unscriptural practice.

(Mark 16:15) *"And he said unto them, Go ye into all the world, and preach the gospel to every creature. (16) He that believeth and is baptized shall be saved; but he that believeth not shall be damned. (17) And these signs shall follow them that believe; In my name shall they cast out devils; they shall speak with new tongues; (18) They shall take up serpents; and if they drink any deadly thing, it shall not hurt them; they shall lay hands on the sick, and they shall recover."* This has been changed to a weak and powerless gospel that has Christians seeking medical relief from worldly physicians, insurance agents, and lawyers. In effect, other signs now follow them that believe their local church teaching: in His name they shall ask Jesus into their heart, enroll in membership, pay tithes, accept many conflicting teachings, not cast out devils, attend Sunday church, participate in programs and classes, and remain in gross ignorance of God's Word. Programs, meetings, and classes have replaced Christ's power in the worldly church.

The Old Testament covenant, in reality a contract between God and a nation of people (Israel), which included the tithe, has been replaced by a new and better, all-nations-and-people covenant. Tithing binds us to the dead letter of the Law, *"the letter killeth,"* rather than the living hope of the promise contained in the new and better covenant that speaks to our giving.

Chapter 7

So You Think You are a TRUE and HONEST TITHER?

Okay, let's say you disagree with this heretical new concept and that you are afraid of *robbing God*. You know tithing was of the Law and before the Law, and Abraham tithed. Let's be honest then and see if you are a true and faithful tither.

Your paycheck and/or your business - do you tithe from the gross or the net? Someone gave you a cake for your birthday, did you carefully measure out a tenth to bring to church? You receive a shirt or pair of shoes for Christmas, your child is given toys, did you let the child choose which toy to give to the ministry and did you tithe from the shoes and shirts? Someone buys your dinner, do you wait until you have received ten purchased meals then take the pastor out to eat? How about that birthday money, Mother's Day flowers, and your garage sale? Did you tithe on all of that? If not, shame on you, you robbed God by withholding your tithe according to the rule of bring *all* the tithe. If someone gave you a car, what are you going to do? Loan it to the pastor every ten days, borrow money to pay a tithe on the value? Did you bring that every third year tithe on your increase which is part of the *all the tithes*? What are we to do? You pay a utility bill, rent, or put gas in the car of a needy brother or sister, do you give them ten percent extra so they can tithe on your gift? If not, you made them a God-robber!

And farmers, pay attention: Leviticus 27:32 - "*And concerning the tithe of the herd, or of the flock, even of whatsoever passeth under the rod, the tenth shall be holy unto the LORD.*" Pastors, start building those livestock pens for the cattle, sheep, chickens, ducks, and *whatsoever* the farmers bring to pay their tithe.

Do your kids tithe of all the Lord God gives them through friends and relatives at all the birthdays, holidays, and graduations? This includes money, clothing, toys, bikes, and whatever. Malachi said *"bring ALL the tithes into the storehouse."* Did you receive increase in those other blessings of food, gifts, and things? How about your tomato plants and lemon tree? You have several choices now: either keep very accurate records so you may tithe of ALL, pray for grace to cover all your sinful God-robbing oversights, give extra just in case, *or...* have the courage to face the truth and admit you cannot keep the law of the tithe.

In some churched families, one member may tithe, another does not. Is the family then cursed? What if unchurched parents buy a son or daughter a car and/or pay for repairs on the vehicle, doesn't the tithe paying adult child owe a tithe on the increase according to *bring ALL the tithes*?

Oh, you say "we are not legalistic" about those things because of grace. But the preacher gets up and teaches the need for ten percent of your paycheck week after week in order for you to be blessed.

So all of those other increases including the produce the livestock, and maybe a vehicle are not important it is just the MONEY we need to be carefully and faithfully tithing?

And what about the church organization itself? Does your church faithfully tithe of ALL that it receives? Then where is the accounting for ALL the donations, clothing, food, bicycles, flowers, meals and don't forget those fund raisers? How can you know for sure that your Church is not robbing God? You may be part of a God-robbing institution and not even know it, and then you get to be partaker of the curse of not keeping the whole law! Or worse, it makes us hypocrites because we say we believe in tithing but fudge or excuse all the little areas where we overlook the need for tithing.

It reminds me of a conversation with a preacher from our old Pentecostal denomination regarding women wearing pants or other apparel *that pertaineth to a man* from Dt. 22:5. When I pointed out that neither he nor his wife had any hesitation or reservations about giving her his jacket, hat, or gloves when the weather was nippy, he replied "but it was cold"! Excuse me, where did Dt.22:5 say manly apparel on a woman was okay when it gets cold?

In one convoluted instance, when my wife was choir director, a question arose in regard to a certain choir member's qualifications. Did she tithe or not? If not, either she was to start tithing now or not return to the choir. It got worse. Her husband, also a church member, did not tithe regularly. Sometimes he would mark *tithe* on the envelope, sometimes *offering*. Was her tithe included too? Since it was not known if this included her tithe, a discussion over this technicality was followed by a meeting with the choir member. Maybe Mt. 6:3 is worth considering here: *"But when thou doest alms, let not thy left hand know what thy right hand doeth, that your alms may be in secret: and thy Father who sees in secret shall recompense thee."* But because the tithe was a requirement for choir membership and leadership, it became an issue.

We even heard we are to tithe of our TIME. God comes first so that would mean a minimum of 2 hours and 24 minutes each day set aside for spiritual works.

Here is the truth: Christ set us free from the Law that no one is truly capable of keeping. You simply cannot keep the

Law and no matter how hard you try, you will fail. This is why we have repented of keeping OT laws and ordinances.

Need we repeat at this stage of this discourse, *tithing was an ordinance of the Law*?

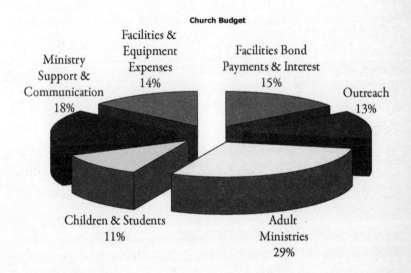

Church Budget

Ministry Support & Communication 18%

Facilities & Equipment Expenses 14%

Facilities Bond Payments & Interest 15%

Outreach 13%

Children & Students 11%

Adult Ministries 29%

Chapter 8

It Really Is More Blessed To Give

In reality, this book is a positive case for cheerful, joyous, Godly, Spirit-directed giving. We find the Bible clearly, repeatedly, throughout the New Testament emphasizes and encourages giving, giving from the heart, give as every man purposes in his own heart; if you see a brother in need, you are to give to him, not just say, "God bless you," and send him away hungry, *"it is more blessed to give," "give and it shall be given unto you."* But we have, in practice, changed it to, *"tithe, and it shall be given unto you, shaken together, pressed down, and running over."* We believe with all of our hearts in giving! When God directs our gifts, we are able to give cheerfully with great joy, especially when we see it is going directly to a specific need in someone's life. Americans are great givers and very generous when they see someone in need or when a disaster strikes. Jesus said we are blessed according to what we give; our seed given is blessed according to what we sow.

As we read the New Testament, charity absolutely abounds in examples of giving and encouragement to give; here is one from Philippians 4:15. *"...when I departed from Macedonia no church communicated with me concerning giving and receiving but you."* (This was a perfect place, by the way, for Paul to quote Malachi and remind the Philippians to tithe as we do.) In 2 Corinthians where Paul instructs on giving, seed sowing, and blessing, he never mentions a tithe; the context is about giving. For anyone to take liberty to insert tithing into his teaching is to add to Scripture (which is absolutely forbidden in Proverbs

30:6, *"...add thou not unto his word lest he reprove thee, and thou be found a liar"* and put a bondage on Christians that hinders the true blessing of purposed, heartfelt giving.

(2 Cor. 9:10) *"Now he that ministereth seed to the sower both minister bread for [your] food, and multiply your seed sown, and increase the fruits of your righteousness); (11) Being enriched in every thing to all bountifulness, which causeth through us thanksgiving to God. (12) For the administration of this service not only supplieth the want (author's note: need) of the saints, but is abundant also by many thanksgivings unto God."*

Where did/do those collections go? To the building fund? To the visiting speaker? Or, maybe we are to tithe first, then support the business of the church, then what is left we give to the needy? This is how it works out in the church system we lived under. But there is a whole 'nother understanding here where the giving is supposed to go.

All the passages quoted here to support tithing and offering, in reality, speak to direct giving to needy saints. Tithing is robbing those in need because the average church-goer is trained to focus his giving into tithes and the weekly offerings to the organizational church. If anything, the poorer church-goer is squeezed to tithe, when what they need to learn is how to give. In fact, Paul strongly encouraged equality and the sharing of our abundance with other saints. This is contrary to the ministerial enrichment, funds-seeking, mega-church, glitz-and-glamour prosperity Christianity on television, and the church buildings all around. The passage about giving *"on the first day of the week as God has prospered you"* in 1 Corinthians 16:1-3 is not about giving to the church, it is about giving to the saints. In nearly 3,000 services I never heard that passage quoted in the context of giving to needy saints!

True Covenant Giving

The true covenant, that God offers to the Church, is found in giving. Does giving put us into a covenant promise with God? "Give and it shall be given unto you" is a specific, direct promise as is the law of sowing and reaping. Are there numerous expressed promises to believers concerning giving we can quote from the New Testament? Of course, and those are true promise covenants God has given us as believers, His promise to bless what we give from our heart (as opposed to keeping a church ordinance, requirement, rule, or legalism). Giving as God specifically directs puts the responsibility on God's children to obey "His commandments" as He speaks to His sheep. This will also, by the way, be one area to test and prove God through the New Testament law of liberty and hearing the voice of the Lord. James wrote, (2:12) "*[D]o, as they that shall be judged by the law of liberty.*"

Understand this, to allow God to speak to us in directing our giving puts a greater responsibility on us in obeying the voice of the Lord. But it also brings us into greater blessing according to His Will for each of us. Maybe it is just time we swallowed hard and confessed we have all robbed God by continuing in something He never told the Church to do.

Can it be that we have robbed God's people of the true blessing of experiencing Holy Spirit-led giving and promised blessing? Maybe there is a real connection to the curse of the Law and areas of our lives such as debt, sickness, afflictions, and other difficulties we face. Is it possible the ministry itself has been robbed by leaning on the law of tithing for support?

Some church leaders even go so far as to call members asking about their tithe on the sale of property or insurance money, and asking to see their paycheck stubs! Tithing is often a requirement for church membership and leadership. Ministers indoctrinate and manipulate both members and leaders to tithe money faithfully, using the Bible and their position of trust and leadership in the name of "being good stewards" and "faithfulness to the kingdom."

Conclusion: There is absolutely no expressed Biblical *covenant* of tithing to the Church of the New Testament, but there are many expressed covenant promises from God regarding giving that never mention a tithe.

And what does God specifically say He will bless? It is giving. He said He would also bless the work of our hands. Do you work with your hands? Are you a giver? Then know and believe God has promised Christians blessings and God keeps His Word. (2 Cor. 9:7) *"Every man according as he purposeth in his heart, [so let him give;] not grudgingly, or of necessity: for God loveth a cheerful giver."* Tithing is not giving. How many times have you heard we must *pay* our tithes?

When we give directly to a brother in need, we are giving directly to Christ Jesus. (Mat. 25:40) *"And the King shall answer and say unto them, Verily I say unto you, Inasmuch as ye have done [it] unto one of the least of these my brethren, ye have done [it] unto me."* (Pro. 19:17) *"He that hath pity upon the poor lendeth unto the LORD; and that which he hath given will he pay him again."*

But according to the church law of the tithe, we are to tithe first, then we can go ahead and give to the needy brother. (Heb. 6:10) *"For God [is] not unrighteous to forget your work and labor of love, which ye have showed toward his name, in that ye have ministered to the saints, and do minister."* The majority of New Testament Scriptural passages which speak of ministering to the saints have to do with giving and sharing with the less fortunate. "*That the rich be careful to maintain good works,*" has everything to do with providing for those in need. But the common church model perverts this teaching to support the organization **first with tithes and offerings**, then, if you have opportunity, you can remember the poor.

Since we have been liberated from the law of tithing, we are more excited about giving than we have ever been, looking to Jesus, the Author and Finisher of our faith, to speak to His sheep where and what to give. We have been more blessed as we are learning to listen to God and give where He directs. It is true! God loves a cheerful giver, and you will love to give when God directs your giving.

So where should a Christian give? Every Christian should begin to ask God, not a man, "Where should I give?" Then go to the Bible and prayerfully pay attention to where God says the giving should go. Expect to hear from the Lord and have the courage to depart from tradition, including the regular Sunday collection habit. You will be amazed to hear God tell you in specific terms to whom and how much to give. You may even end up meeting the unspoken needs of God's people, and be blessed accordingly, as you rejoice in helping a brother or sister in need!

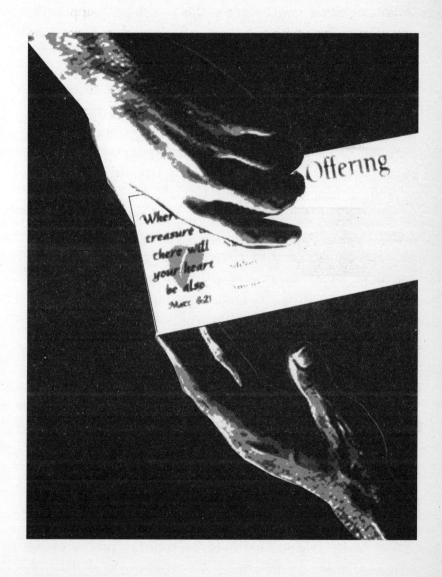

Chapter 9

Paul Assumed Tithing For Us?

Yes, we can agree the early Jewish Christian church tithed, kept the Sabbath, and offered gifts and sacrifices under the Law. But by 70 A.D., with the destruction of Jerusalem and the temple, those practices were over. Long before that event, however, Paul had written apostolic letters to churches clarifying the laws and ordinances in the New Testament, never once reminding them to tithe or keep the Sabbath. So how may we assume the early Church tithed and then make that firm doctrine? In the New Testament, regarding tithing, there is no stated example given of any church bringing or giving tithes. To assume or use human reasoning that tithing "was an accepted custom" or that tithing is "a starting point for giving" is to go beyond what the Bible actually says and add an unexpressed rule or standard into Scripture where there is none. This is human reasoning at best and adding cursed leaven to Scripture at worst.

Darkness or Light?

(Psa. 119:105) *"Thy word [is] a lamp unto my feet, and a light unto my path."* Someone says the Christian church tithed with no Scripture telling it to or saying it did? Then you have no lamp for your feet and no light for your path to walk therein as you follow that teaching. This is walking in darkness without His Word.

Many early non-Jewish believers had no previous experience or knowledge of tithing. Acts 10:2 speaks of the Gentile Italian centurion, Cornelius, describing him as, *"A devout [man], and one that feared God with all his house, which gave much alms to the people, and prayed to God always."* According to Scripture, Cornelius, a devout man, was mentioned as a giver, not a tither.

As the Word of God grew and non-Jews were added to the Church, Paul was passionate in his concern about them not taking on Jewish customs and legalisms. Galatians and Colossians specifically address Christians being free in Christ from the laws and ordinances of the Old Covenant.

Isaiah 28:9-10 tells how doctrine is built, *"For precept [must be] upon precept, precept upon precept; line upon line, line upon line; here a little, [and] there a little,"* from Scripture, never from assumptions and never from an absence of command and example. Anyone making an assumption about doctrine apart from the Scripture, opens wide the door for error, deception, and corruption.

In our old church we were taught tithing from the example of Abraham in Hebrews 8, apparently after the pastor realized that tithing was of the Law, also. He had unintentionally been mis-teaching for years by using the Law and prophets. Unscriptural phrases such as, *"tithing is where our giving should begin,"* and, *"because God owns it all we should tithe,"* are used to influence the Church. Wrestling the Scriptures to fit a tradition inherited from religion is common in the Christian world and most of us have stumbled by repeating someone else's error. Once you remove the teeth of the Law of Moses and the prophets to Israel from the tithe teaching, you are left with an unscriptural case based on custom, tradition, and a <u>church's need of funding</u>.

Over the years we heard far more teaching on tithing and offerings than on faith, healing, heaven, hell, or baptism.

About twenty-five to thirty percent of the membership faithfully tithed to the ministry and gave offerings to the church (most of which paid for church overhead). Now we realize we were, in reality, funding a government-licensed 501c3 corporation operating as a ministry, rather than giving to the real Church, the Body of Christ!

That is not to completely discount all church corporations or say all are evil or wrong, because a lot of good is done by many great ministries, as exemplified by James Dobson's Focus on the Family and others. The error is that the typical member has no idea his church is a government-licensed corporation and that the real Church of Jesus Christ is the body of believers, not the business or institution. (By the way, Dr. Dobson's Focus on the Family ministry has been greatly impacted by the 501c3 laws and IRS in their ability to speak out publicly on social issues.)

We are personally aware of the corruption of God's servants by money, resulting in the creation of corporate church hirelings living off the sheep. With the one-man-pastor-CEO style of leadership, there are many opportunities for Satan to use money from tithes and church salaries to wreak havoc in the life of church leaders. Examples we know of abound, not just in the large, visible televangelist world, but in countless small churches in small towns.

After a quarter century of association with church groups who taught and enforced a rule of tithing, we now realize how the leadership suffers and is led astray by this. Tithing fosters a judgmental and self-righteous attitude in both ministers and members. Tithing creates an expectation of financial reward and/or gain; an error that further leads to manipulation by church leaders in the form of membership requirements.

In one church consisting of around 250 members, including mainly working middle-class people, a bishop commented to the pastor, "See those people out there? Those are your CDs" (certificates of deposit savings accounts).

Another former pastor illegally borrowed church funds for personal purchases and lived an extravagant ministerial lifestyle while members sold peanut brittle to fundraise for the church. Visiting ministers were well fed at fine restaurants, and monthly getaways were common for the *resting* of the ministry.

A church leader and his wife were once lifted up as great people of God after a $250,000 offering they raised in one service out-of-state while pastoring a church there. They were also closely monitoring who tithed and how much, to the point of calling people asking how soon they were going to bring in the tithe. In one example, this included calling a newly widowed woman for her tithe in an insurance death-of-spouse settlement!

Some years ago, two gifted prophets, who taught tithing and ministered to our church, actually argued with each other over who got the best offering from our church, boasting of how much they were paid!

Stories have surfaced of local Christian ministers taking trips and other gambling spots for vacations and recreation-away from the eyes of their congregations who tithe to them. In church, the tithe is holy when it is taken on Sunday. Is it still holy when laid down as a bet on the tables of Las Vegas?

I could list many more personal examples from an insider's position as we were part of church leadership and knew many ministers from tithing churches, both independent and denominational. Over that period of time we saw in many ministers an indulgent ministerial lifestyle while members fund-raised for the church, and, faithfully, with no questions asked, supported our leaders with our tithes.

Tithing was required for any leadership in our former *grace* church of approximately 150 members (including teachers, choir, musicians, etc.) The pastor had sole control and there was no accountability of the tithe income account, which funded his ministry and lifestyle; offerings and fundraisers supported the church operation and overhead. To his credit, when the church was small, the pastor sacrificed his own funds (from the tithe) in order to keep the church operation viable during the lean times of the startup years, and he personally helped many people generously with needs through the years. As the church grew, his personal lifestyle adapted to the prosperity of the church: daily meals at restaurants, travel, etc., became an integral part of the ministry and visiting ministers were well-paid (large financial gifts, air fare, golf games, hotels, and expensive meals included) to speak in our church. These speakers were touted as "life-changing", "next level," "cutting edge," "big time" ministries who would powerfully lift up the church. One of them we know of was paid $2,000 for one weekend service. Another evangelist was paid in cash, offerings and perks of over $41,000 during a period of four months. Both of these speakers were being paid quite generously at a rate very few in the congregation could earn on their jobs.

From an insider's position, we saw the ministry write off, as church expense, much of their personal expenses. Vacations, travel, books, phone, meals, auto expenses, clothing, babysitters, housekeepers, and home repairs are routinely written off as ministry expenses in the professional clergy. Church members often provide free labor and services for the privileged clergy. In one personal instance, we recall how church members re-roofed the pastor's home, and we know these are typical actions of sincere, loving church members. Sort of makes you want to aspire to the ministry, doesn't it?

When you compare these examples with what Paul said of his ministry, the leaven and mammon of which Christ warned, and read of what Peter reminded leaders, we have red lights and siren alarms as to where the church has strayed. (1 Pet. 5:2) *"Feed the flock of God which is among you, taking the oversight [thereof], not by constraint, but willingly; not for filthy lucre (author's note: pay), but of a ready mind."*

Now let's read some interesting things about Paul's ministry you've probably never heard. Paul said in 1 Corinthians 9:18, *"What is my reward then? [verily] that, when I preach the gospel, I may make the gospel of Christ without charge, that I abuse not my power in the gospel."* Remember that the next time your church membership comes to you selling chicken dinners, raffles, or peanut brittle, or holding yard sales, or asking for donations *for the church*. Many times church staff and visiting ministers eat at fine restaurants courtesy of the good folks in the pews. This is common practice in the church world today, and, in our case, we assumed this was the way the ministry was to operate as we followed our leaders.

Paul said in 2 Corinthians 2:17, *"For we are not as many, which corrupt the word of God: but as of sincerity, but as of God, in the sight of God speak we in Christ."* Corrupt in Strong's is number 2585 and means *to retail*. "We have some books and CDs for you to purchase out in the lobby, folks, and at the other table you can buy tickets for the chicken dinner. Later we will take a special offering for pastor's vacation and Saturday is the church yard sale for the remodel fund." Sound familiar? If you hang around the evangelical church world for long, it is a guaranteed experience.

Paul's Example To The Whole Church

Paul the apostle worked when he preached and ministered in churches. Paul said he worked to set an example to the church at Ephesus in Acts 20:34-35; this example he gave was for the pastors, teachers, elders, and evangelists! The Scripture testimony of Paul confesses he worked while at Thessalonica, Ephesus, and Corinth. (Acts 18:3) *"And because he was of the same craft, he abode with them, and wrought: for by their occupation they were tentmakers."* Three of the early churches bear witness to the fact this apostle of Jesus was not a salaried or tithe-taking minister. Paul never requested an offering or tithe for himself, unlike the high-paid televangelists, healers, and many preachers. In fact, he told the church at Thessalonica, *"If any work not, neither should he eat."* The pastors are included in the *any*.

Paul At Corinth

(1 Cor. 9:18) *"that I preach the gospel without charge."* In 1 Corinthians 9:6 and 9:14 Paul affirms that even though he and Barnabbas had the power *"to forebear working"* and that *"they which preach the gospel should live of the gospel,"* in verse 15 he declares, *"But I have used none of these things: neither have I written...that it should be so done unto me."* What? No $1,000 speaking fees? No tithes? No perks?

He said he would rather die than take from those Christians. (1 Cor. 9:15) *"But I have used none of these things: neither have I written these things, that it should be so done unto me: for [it were] better for me to die, than that any man should make my glorying void."*

78

This was not a short visit; he stayed at Corinth ministering for one-and-one-half years (Acts 18:11). By his third trip to Corinth, the elderly Paul was supplied by other brethren. (2 Cor. 11:7) *"Have I committed an offence in abasing myself that ye might be exalted, because I have preached to you the gospel of God freely? (8) I robbed other churches, taking wages [of them] to do you service. (9) And when I was present with you, and wanted, I was chargeable to no man: for that which was lacking to me the brethren which came from Macedonia supplied: and in all [things] I have kept myself from being burdensome unto you, and [so] will I keep [myself]."* Again, no mention of tithes or taking offerings for himself. God supplied his needs through willing brethren; he went by faith and his needs were met. God is able to speak to other believers to help those He sends. He is a good God!

Paul At Ephesus

Paul said likewise to the church elders and overseers (apostles, pastors, teachers, prophets, elders) at Ephesus. (Acts 20:17) *"[H]e sent to Ephesus, and called the elders of the church (28) over the which the Holy Ghost hath made you overseers (34) Yea, ye yourselves know, that these hands have ministered unto my necessities, and to them that were with me. (35) I have showed you all things, how that so laboring ye ought to support the weak, and to remember the words of the Lord Jesus, how he said, It is more blessed to give than to receive."*

Paul At Thessalonica

(2 Ths. 3:7) *"For yourselves know how ye ought to imitate us: for we behaved not ourselves disorderly among you; (8) Neither did we eat any man's bread for nothing; but wrought with labour and travail night and day, that we might not be chargeable*

79

to any of you: (9) Not because we have not power, but to make ourselves an ensample unto you to follow us. (10) For even when we were with you, this we commanded you, that if any would not work, neither should he eat."

Paul's word and example to three churches speaks strong and loud. Not only should they not be taking tithes and offerings, many should be working to support the weak and needy members! This is exactly what Paul wrote and told to the overseers of the flock at Ephesus. Ministers who are truly called of God to serve will be provided for by God.

Some assume Paul and others lived from the tithe. Paul specifically said that he worked as an example to all in those churches! No paid preacher, no paid hierarchy, no paid staff, no paid corporate organization, no advertising, no fundraising.

In a related passage in Philippians 3:7, he said, "*brethren* (author's note: the minister's were included, of course), *become imitators together of me, and mark them that so walk...even as you have us for an example.*"

Consider 2 Thessalonians 3:7-12 in regard to imitating the ministry of Paul. *(7)"For yourselves know how ye ought to imitate us: for we behaved not ourselves disorderly among you; (8) Neither did we eat any man's bread for nothing; but wrought with labour and travail night and day, that we might not be chargeable to any of you: (9) Not because we have not power, but to make ourselves an ensample unto you to follow us. (10) For even when we were with you, this we commanded you, that if any would not work, neither should he eat. (11) For we hear that there are some which walk among you disorderly, working not at all, but are busybodies. (12) Now them that are such we command and exhort by our Lord Jesus Christ, that with quietness they work, and eat their own bread."*

Does your church leadership imitate Paul in this Scripture passage?

Do you have any verse where Paul took tithes for the clergy to imitate?

Paul did receive gifts to minister to the needy saints in other churches, but never for a building program or church building furnishing.

In the New Testament, where do you find the collections, gifts, and contributions going?

Are we to allow error and withhold truth for fear that a brother will stumble? (Rom. 16:17-18) "*Now I beseech you, brethren, mark them that are causing the divisions and occasions of stumbling, contrary to the doctrine which ye learned* (author's note: Paul never taught a doctrine of tithing)*: and turn away from them. For they that are such serve not our Lord Christ, but their own belly; and by their smooth and fair speech they beguile the hearts of the innocent.*"

Is it not amazing that Paul wrote fourteen books of the New Testament addressed to churches and individuals and there is absolute silence in regard to paying or giving a tithe to Paul or his associates?

When Paul Went Full Time

This came when Paul was supported by the provision of God through believers. As Jesus had experienced in the last three years of His life and ministry, Paul's needs were met. He no longer worked with his hands as he ministered, nor did the other apostles when they forsook their craft in order to pray and study God's Word. (Acts 6:2,4) "*Then the twelve called the multitude of the disciples [unto them], and said, It is not reason that we should leave the word of God, and serve tables. But we will give ourselves continually to prayer, and to the ministry of the word.*"

There is no mention of being supported by the tithes here.

In Philippians 4:15-17, Paul had a need and wrote to them in the matter of *"giving and receiving,"* again, a perfect place to mention a tithe if he wanted to do so. *"[W]hen I departed from Macedonia, no church communicated with me as concerning giving and receiving, but ye only. (18) For even in Thessalonica ye sent once and again unto my necessity. (17) Not because I desire a gift...."*

This passage, quoted earlier, reflects Paul's view of God's provision for His workers. (1 Cor. 9:6-12) *"Or I only and Barnabas, have not we power to forebear working? (7) Who goeth a warfare any time at his own charges? who planteth a vineyard, and eateth not of the fruit thereof? or who feedeth a flock, and eateth not of the milk of the flock? (8) Say I these things as a man? or saith not the law the same also? (9) For it is written in the law of Moses, though shalt not muzzle the mouth of the ox that treadeth out the corn. Doth God take care for oxen? (10) Or saith he [it] altogether for our sakes? For our sakes, not doubt, [this] is written: that he that ploweth should plow in hope: and that he that thresheth in hope should be partaker of his hope. (11) If we have sown unto you spiritual things, [is it] a great thing if we shall reap your carnal things? (12) If others be partakers of [this] power over you, [are] not we rather? Nevertheless we have not used this power; but suffer all things, lest we should hinder the gospel of Christ."*

Here, Paul made the case for God's ministers partaking of the fruit of the vineyard in which they labor (without mentioning tithes, quoting Malachi, or referring to Abraham's tithe).

Another place Paul mentions his needs being met (again without a mention of the tithe) is Philippians 2:25. *"Yet I sup-*

posed it necessary to send to you Epaphroditus, my brother, and companion in labour, and fellowsoldier, but your messenger, and he that ministered to my wants. (29) Receive him therefore in the Lord with all gladness; and hold such in reputation: (30) Because for the work of Christ he was nigh unto death, not regarding his life, to supply your lack of service toward me."

David Eells writes in Chapter 19 of <u>Sovereign God For Us and Through Us</u>:

"Early in our discipleship, we began to walk by faith for God to be our supplier so that when we went from part-time to full-time ministry it was natural to continue these methods. We have never taken up offerings (an oxymoron), told people our needs, preached gimmee sermons, borrowed money, taken government benefits, or worked at a secular job. I am not saying this to brag, but to show God's power to provide without these methods. I also had to go this way to be qualified to teach on this subject. The Apostle Paul said, (Rom. 15:18) *'For I will not dare to speak of any things save those which Christ wrought through me, for the obedience of the Gentiles, by word and deed, (19) in the power of signs and wonders, in the power of the Holy Spirit.'*

"Years ago the Lord told me, 'I am sending you through a wilderness so that you can tell my people that I still supply in the wilderness.' As you can imagine, this lifestyle put us in many situations to prove His promises. The Lord wanted me to be able to speak from experience about His sovereignty to *'supply your every need, according to His riches in glory,'* without resorting to the legalistic manipulations that *Christendom* normally resorts to. He said, *'Freely ye received, freely give.'*

"We have received only freewill offerings sent from God through those that He spoke to. I would not have traded these wilderness experiences for anything, for they have totally impressed me with my Father. We have worked diligently in the Lord's service, and He said the *'laborer is worthy of his hire.'* My pay comes from Him. This also keeps us free from the manipulations of man."

The Widow's Mite illustration by Gustave Dore.
(Mark 12:41-44) *And Jesus sat over against the treasury, and beheld how the people cast money into the treasury: an many that were rich cast in much. (42) And there came a certain poor widow, and she threw in two mites, which make a farthing. (43) And he called unto him his disciples, and saith unto them, Verily I say unto you, That this poor widow hath cast more in, than all they which have cast into the treasury. (44) For all they did cast in of their abundance; but she of her want did cast in all that she had, even all her living.*

Chapter 10

True Authority

Pastors and ministers have no Biblical authority to receive tithes in the New Testament, as contrasted with the Levites, who were commanded under the Law to receive them! Hebrews 7:5 is explicit on this point. No pastor or minister holds the Levitical priesthood office, hence, no tithes. The same passage in Hebrews 7:11 says the priesthood was changed. *"If therefore perfection were by the Levitical priesthood, (for under it the people received the law,) what further need [was there] that another priest should rise after the order of Melchisedec, and not be called after the order of Aaron? (12) For the priesthood being changed, there is made of necessity a change also of the law."*

If you still want to tithe, your church and minister should openly be accountable to you for their tithe, for they are not above the Law they teach.

Have you asked why just the pastor is collecting the tithes? The Bible gave a five-fold ministry of apostles, prophets, evangelists, teachers and pastors. (Eph. 4:11) *"And he gave some, apostles; and some, prophets; and some, evangelists; and some, pastors and teachers; (12) For the perfecting of the saints, for the work of the ministry, for the edifying of the body of Christ."* Compare this again with Nehemiah 13:5, *"and the tithes of the corn, the new wine, and the oil, which was commanded [to be given] to the Levites, and the singers, and the porters."*

In our church, only the pastor collected the tithes (which was mentioned from the pulpit almost every week). If there is a Biblical five-fold ministry in the local church, shouldn't they

-apostles, prophets, evangelists, teachers, pastors- all take their share of the tithe? Attention Sunday School teachers!

Do you see how far from Scriptural Christianity we have fallen? There is no Biblical model of the pastor-CEO style of leadership, as we observe so commonly. Pastors have not a single verse of Scripture giving them authority to take tithes from anyone. The world would be a lot better off if Christians exercised the authority Jesus gave His disciples in Matthew 10:1. *"And when he had called unto [him] his twelve disciples, he gave them power [against] unclean spirits, to cast them out, and to heal all manner of sickness and all manner of disease."*

The real travesty is in the number of churches exercising power and authority over other people's money, rather than over the works of the devil! It is painfully obvious we have created a kingdom of paid ministers, while not bringing baby Christians to maturity so that they walk in the authority and power of the Word Christ gave believers.

Remember, there is a role model, an example from Scripture for one man taking the ten percent. (1 Sam. 8:15) "And he will take the tenth of your seed, and of your vineyards, and give to his officers, and to his servants. (17) He will take the tenth of your sheep: and ye shall be his servants." His name was King Saul. He started out as a Godly, humble, servant of God.

Am I saying every tithe-taking minister is like that corrupt Saul back in 1 Samuel? No, not every one of them, although I have met quite a few over the years and the majority were corrupted to one degree or another. I have known some sincere ministers, who really did care for and want the best for their flocks, but, honestly, they were in the minority. The system, like the Old Testament people of God who wanted a king, has a way of blinding and corrupting good men who love God.

Ministers who take tithes and salaries without the clear example or command of the Lord are not living the Christian faith they teach. (Mt. 10:8) *"Heal the sick, cleanse the lepers, raise the dead, cast out devils: freely ye received, freely give. (9) Provide neither gold, nor silver, nor brass in your purses."* We have it backwards; we give ministers the gold and silver while most of them fail to heal the sick, cast out devils, etc.! If a man is sent by God, God will see that he is provided for. If a man cannot walk by faith, he is not sent by God. But when you look at the church world around us and give consideration to God's Word regarding the matter, you get a vastly different picture of church giving.

Under the tithe-salary system, the pastor becomes an employee, as he is paid for his services. This is contrary to the New Testament, and the shocking statistics of ministerial burn-out and failure is testimony that something is seriously wrong with the church system around us. Because the typical evangelical church is incorporated, owns property, and has departments and staff, the typical pastor becomes the manager-administrator-CEO of an organization. What if the average pastor simply worked, as Paul admonished the elders and overseers to do, and had church meetings in homes without the complexities of a church-business? Can a man honestly minister effectively to 100 people from a pulpit in a building, or could he minister more effectively in a home with five to twenty people? Given the current mass exodus out of big-box churches into home churches, the answer may be self-evident.

It is an unscriptural authority ministers use to teach tithing to the Church. If you have God's Word, you speak with His authority. Tithing has no such word or authority in the Church. That is why every man who teaches the law or rule of tithing has already been corrupted, whether he knows it or not. The tithe corrupts the ministry by subtlety with the expectation the people need to tithe and contribute to their church.

Neither does the Bible say "tithing is a starting place for giving." This is human reasoning and apostate, meaning fallen away from the truth. God's Word is truth and authority.

Paul speaks the shocking truth to the Corinthians when he compares his ministry, in which he preaches the gospel without charge, to the false apostles and ministers, who take pay for their ministry. (2 Cor. 11:7) *"Have I committed an offence in abasing myself* (author's note: by not taking pay) *that ye might be exalted, because I have preached to you the gospel of God freely? (8) I robbed other churches, taking wages [of them], to do you service. (9) And when I was present with you, and wanted, I was chargeable to no man: for that which was lacking to me the brethren which came from Macedonia supplied: and in all [things] I have kept myself from being burdensome unto you, and [so] will I keep my[self]. (10) As the truth of Christ is in me, no man shall stop me of this boasting in the regions of Achaia. (11) Wherefore? because I love you not? God knoweth. (12) But what I do, that I will do, that I may cut off occasion from them which desire occasion* (author's note: meaning opportunity, from Strong's number 874); *that wherein they glory, they may be found even as we* (author's note: unpaid ministers of the Gospel). *(13) For such* (author's note: ministers who take opportunity) *[are] false apostles, deceitful workers, transforming themselves into the apostles of Christ. (14) And no marvel; for Satan himself is transformed into an angel of light. (15) Therefore [it is] no great thing if his ministers also be transformed as the ministers of righteousness; whose end shall be according to their works."* This is the system God is calling his ministers out of; the harlot church of Revelation 18.

Chapter 11

Blessings and Curses

Testimonies abound of tithers who are blessed financially, of that there is no dispute. However, may we add that tithers tend to also be givers, for whom God has indeed directly promised His blessing. Could it be that they are indeed blessed through the open window of giving, and not because of obedience to a church ordinance of tithing?

At the same time we see many tithers experiencing blessing, we also see a great number of tithers in debt and many tithers living in poverty. Credit cards, car payments, housing, and personal debt abound in the Christian church today. Apparently, many tithers have no reservations about borrowing to finance abundant life, yet Scripture says borrowing is one of the curses of the Law! (Dt. 28:44) *"He shall lend to thee, and thou shalt not lend to him: he shall be the head, and thou shalt be the tail. (45) Moreover all these curses shall come upon thee, and shall pursue thee, and overtake thee, till thou be destroyed; because thou hearkenedst not unto the voice of the LORD thy God, to keep his commandments and his statutes which he commanded thee: (46) and they shall be upon thee for a sign and for a wonder, and upon thy seed for ever."*

Debt is one of the curses of the Law in operation according to Deuteronomy 28. How many tithers have debt? How many churches with a tithing rule have corporate debt? The borrower is still bond servant to the lender, according to the Law. And yet they borrow to finance a building, organization, and kingdom that appears successful to man. But not God.

Another reason we have been taught to tithe, is that, in order for God to bless us, we needed to be faithful in our tithing. Yet among the church-goers, and those we knew were tithers, sickness and accident were just as common (in some cases more so) than those of the non-tithers. Sickness is specifically mentioned as a manifestation of the curse in Deuteronomy 28. Have you ever wondered why so many Christians are plagued with sickness, which, according to Scripture, is part of the curse?

One woman complained of her husband's $900 monthly drug bill that the insurance would not pay. Was the blessing or curse at work, was the *devourer* being rebuked? Yet, they religiously taught in their church the tithe-to-be-blessed doctrine.

Another elderly couple was routinely given the responsibility of speaking to the congregation, encouraging them to tithe, yet, they were some of the most ill and afflicted people we knew.

Some time ago, a Christian left this world. At the funeral, he was remembered as a "faithful tither." But he left his wife with debt, underinsured, and unable to keep their home. What was the weightier matter, a faithful tithe or providing for his own? At his funeral it was said how he faithfully kept his church's teaching on tithing. But he missed the voice of the Shepherd in making sure his spouse was provided for. He had learned to keep a teaching on the tithe, yet, never learned the faith to believe God for healing (for which the New Testament abounds in promises). They missed the blessing that he was taught tithing would bring him. The devourer was not rebuked, even though he faithfully tithed.

In our years of experience we have observed an amazing pattern of sickness, disease, and affliction in the membership of those churches who emphasized the need to tithe. (Dt. 28:60) *"Moreover he will bring upon thee all the diseases of Egypt, which thou wast afraid of; and they shall cleave unto thee. (61) Also every sickness, and every plague, which [is] not written in the book of this law, them will the LORD bring upon thee, until thou be destroyed." (Gal. 3:10) "For as many as are of the works of the law are under the curse: for it is written, Cursed is every one that continueth not in all things which are written in the book of the law to do them."*

It is error and deception to say we do not keep the Law because of grace and Abraham tithed before the Law, so we should tithe likewise. God put tithing in the Law, and the fact that the diseases of Egypt prevail in God's people bear witness to the curse at work, just as Paul told the Galatians. Can anyone connect the dots here?

Indeed, Scripture says the Law severs us from Christ (*"making Christ of no effect"*) in Galatians. Church rules, legalisms, and ordinances make it easy to fall from grace, which is unearned favor with God. God never promised the Church a blessing if they tithed, He promised His blessing on those that give willingly, as a man purposes in his heart, and/or when the Lord directs.

Regardless, which rule of the Law we observe, whether tithing, Sabbath-keeping, dress codes, etc., we have fallen from grace regarding that matter because righteousness is not of the Law. It becomes a snare, and our giving may then become moved by human emotion, fleshly recognition, good intentions, greed, fear, clergy manipulation, or other motives from the soulish realm and not from God. No wonder Christians are so easily deceived into making bad financial decisions, and no wonder so many clergymen are corrupted by financial expectation.

In 1991, when we were still members of a highly legalistic Pentecostal group, the Word of the Lord came in some of the most profound words the Lord has ever spoken to me: *"The paint on Jezebel's face is nothing compared to the paint of man's righteousness with which you have covered over the face of God."*

Those words both frightened me and directly challenged my Christian belief system which followed our denominational statement! He was speaking of the religious practices that we thought were holy, righteous, and God-pleasing, but they were leaven, full of legalisms, and I trembled to think of how we had misrepresented God to others.

Our own church experience also bears witness to this. We have tithed about 98% of the time over the last twenty-four years. About fourteen years ago, while we were members of that highly legalistic organization, we had tithed ten percent and five percent offering consistently. During this time we were given a new home, debt-free. But because of the church requirement of tithe and offering, we mortgaged our home and paid a $16,000 tithe and $8,000 offering to *the storehouse*. Twelve years later, we have mortgage debt. Has God been good to us? Absolutely! We have been healed, blessed, and provided for; however, debt has nagged us the whole time.

Borrowing and debt are among the curses of the Law and even though we kept the law of the tithe, we were guilty of not continuing in all of the Law, so the curse of debt was freely able to operate, even after we became part of a grace church. (Gal. 3:10) *"For as many as are of the works of the law are under the curse: for it is written, Cursed is every one that continueth not in all things which are written in the book of the law to do them."* If you are a tither, you need to re-read that verse because tithing is in the Law, as we have abundantly shown from Scripture. Please read Deuteronomy 28 and see what the curse is: you owe it to yourself and your family.

If your church teaches tithing, they must of necessity say the early Church did also, yet there is no Biblical record of any church or saint tithing. So how can anyone still affirm the practice of tithing based on the lack of Biblical record?

It is a dilemma: if you say the early Church believed in tithing when there is no Biblical command to do so, you have added to Scripture, which is forbidden in Revelation 22 under the penalty of the curse for adding to the words of His books. If you admit there is no Biblical record of Christians or churches tithing, then you are creating a rule or legalism for which God gives you no authority in Scripture. Jesus called this "*leaven of the Pharisees.*" You are guilty of adding to the New Testament Scripture if you say the early Church tithed with no verses to back it up.

After receiving this understanding from the Lord and repenting for keeping the law that Christ set us free of, we began to ask God to specifically direct us in giving. A remarkable thing immediately began to take place. The Lord spoke a specific amount to give to a ministry, then after a few days, He spoke another amount to give to another ministry, each time giving my wife and me the same dollar figure without prior thought, discussion, or consultation.

There were times when God specifically directed us to give an amount, and on several occasions, our vehicle. One year we gave away two cars to needy Christians, and God, in turn, blessed us with a brand new Ford F-150 Super Cab truck given to our family. "*Give and it shall be given...*" operated wonderfully in our lives and we were blessed, indeed, and gave joyfully.

If that were not enough indication we were on the right path, the Lord gave us each yet another matching amount to give to yet another ministry, again, without prior thought, or discussion. For this, we praise and magnify the Lord, our Joy. This pattern is now repeating itself in our giving; God speaks where and how much, and we respond from the storehouse over which we are stewards.

One morning God impressed me to sow into Eastern Europe. We have no connections there and didn't know anyone from that part of the world. Amazingly, an hour later when talking to my Christian friend, J.I., in another city, he told me they just had dinner with a missionary to Lithuania who worked with orphaned children. The poverty is so profound some parents abandon their children to orphanages. We gave to that work the amount He told us to give. Praise God! This is the fruit of the truth. He has directed us in giving, to whom and how much, and we are so blessed to hear Him so clearly and obey His command! This is joyful, heartfelt giving, and not the obligatory duty of tithing.

Chapter 12

A Better Covenant

It is a distinctly human trait to cling tenaciously to long held conceptions of truth and once challenged will eventually relinquish these beliefs only by passing through three separate phases, known as the *three stages of truth*. During the first stage, the issue goes unnoticed and is ignored. Everyone accepts and goes along without question. The second state is characterized by a period of vehement denial, argument, and challenge. The third stage witnesses the clear certainty about the issue being finally recognized as self-evident.

While writing this book, after prayer and study, as we slowly realized there is no directive in Scripture for Christian tithing, we personally experienced those three stages. As we began to search the Scriptures, we asked ourselves over and over, "How can this be?" After all, we had been taught tithing and practiced the same for more than two decades! How could our good pastor and other church leaders be wrong? But as the truth emerged from studying Scripture, we realized again the church teaching was wrong at best, and put us back under the curse of the law at worst.

The negative effects of tithing are numerous:
- *Tithing teaches Christians that God gets ten percent; they get to keep the rest and are stewards over ninety percent.*
- *Tithing brings believers back under the law and the curse.*
- *Tithing tends to corrupt leaders and gives many an expectation that the tithe is owed to their ministry.*
- *Tithing takes from the poor whom the Church is called to help.*

- *Tithing diverts and perverts Scriptural giving into church corporations.*
- *Tithing brings condemnation and defiles the conscience of Christians.*
- *Tithing is not giving from the heart; it is an act of obedience to an erroneous and religious teaching.*
- *Tithing fosters a judgmental attitude toward those who do not tithe.*
- *Tithing veils the spiritual vision of the believer.*

For well over a year the Lord has added line upon line, precept upon precept, to this study. He is the One Who called and anointed us to write this, for "it is the honor of kings to search out a matter," and again, 1 John 2:27 says, "*But the anointing which ye have received of Him abideth in you, and ye need not that any man teach you: but as the same anointing teacheth you of all things, and is truth, and is no lie, and even as it hath taught you, ye shall abide in Him.*" John 14:26 speaks of the Holy Spirit teaching us and bringing Scripture to our remembering. Not to rebel, not to undermine, not to divide, but to establish truth in the Body of Christ and destroy yokes.

The ongoing exposure of extravagant, worldly ministerial lifestyles bears witness to the fact that the institutional Christian church system is corrupted nearly beyond hope. The mass exodus away from the institutional church is justified and God is doing it. In fact, George Barna recently wrote <u>Revolution</u>, a fascinating book about this movement away from the institutional church.

In our case, we had to leave the church in order to find the Church! It is remarkable that the largest growth of Christianity is to the house church, and that is where God has led us, also. We gather with a wonderful small group of people in love and fellowship without overhead, fundraising, tithes, staff meetings, or dry, repetitive, formal orchestrated services.

Several weeks after beginning this book and receiving this understanding from God's Word, I heard David Eells interviewed on Christian radio. The host mentioned Christians need to support the ministry and tithing. However, as I listened, Brother Eells gently corrected the program host on his tithing belief. I called my wife and said, "Hey! This guy is talking about the same thing God has shown us!"

Another tactic is to put God's people under the Law to support them (the clergy) when the Scripture clearly states that our giving is *"not of necessity."* (2 Cor. 9:7) *"[Let] each man [do] according as he has purposed in his heart (author's note: not according to Law): not grudgingly, or of necessity (author's note: not according to Law): for God loveth a cheerful giver."* In the New Testament, God wants an offering from the heart from those born of His Spirit. God made the Old covenant with the Jews, not the Church. If a doctrine, such as tithing, is not in the New Covenant, then it was never made with you!

Jesus, rebuking those under the Old Covenant, said in Matthew 23:23, *"Woe unto you, scribes and Pharisees, hypocrites! for ye tithe mint and anise and cumin* (author's note: even their seasonings), *and have left undone the weightier matters of the law, justice and mercy, and faith: but these you ought to have done* (author's note: past tense in all ancient manuscripts and the Received Text), *and not to have left the other undone."*

The purpose of this book is to prove Scripturally the truth that tithing is not for New Covenant Christians as has been commonly taught. The New Testament promise of blessing is according to Scriptural giving as expressly written to the Church of God:

(Lk. 6:38) "*Give, and it shall be given unto you; good measure, pressed down, and shaken together, and running over, shall men give into your bosom. For with the same measure that ye mete withal it shall be measured to you again.*"

(2 Cor. 9:7) "*Every man according as he purposeth in his heart, [so let him give]; not grudgingly, or of necessity: for God loveth a cheerful giver.*"

Simply put, the Old Testament with the law of the tithe was done away with as it was fulfilled in Christ. The "*better covenant*" of the New Testament gives us the grace of the higher and better way through our giving. The true giving to Melchizedek, a type of Christ, is not when you tithe or give to the church institution; it is when "*you have done it to the least of these, your brethren, you have done it unto me,*" as Jesus said.

Yes, we have robbed God, but not as some ministers teach. We have robbed God by not giving as the Bible speaks. By denying the ministry "*to the saints*" in giving, we have not only robbed God but by our ignorance literally caused people to perish. "*My people perish for lack of knowledge*" (the Scriptural knowledge of true Biblical giving). In the church system all around us and in the media, the vast majority of funding is swallowed up by church programs, overhead, salaries, and tithes. Only a fraction of total giving to these institutional churches goes where it is Scripturally directed. The tithe is Old Testament Law. We are no longer owners of anything, but stewards of that with which our Father has blessed us. We now give as God directs, give willfully by choice, and give as we "*purpose in our hearts.*"

These stories and experiences related are not written to hurt, rail against, or accuse anyone. These illustrations are part of our Christian experience and what we learned from them.

99

We are all in a battle with the flesh and easily led astray. The examples given are principle-driven illustrations of how *lucre* can influence, corrupt, and *deceive even the elect* in good churches. As such, they are now *working to the good* in our lives and we bear no ill-will or malice toward anyone from our former churches.

As we read His Word, we have noted how different the modern church is from the ministry of Jesus and the book of Acts. Every week has brought Scriptural insight and revelation, much of which we were never taught or heard from a pulpit. God has shown us *hidden manna* regarding the error of teaching tithing to Christians. We found that the corollary to the church and money was found between the institutional church, which cries out for money to build buildings and organizations, versus the Biblical Church in Acts that encouraged work, giving, and supporting the poor and needy while meeting in homes.

Scripture also shows Paul working and teaching Christians, including ministers, to work and help support the poor so that there would be equality. The tithe-taking churches and ministers take from the poor in the name of "you will be blessed." We are personally convinced the system of the institutional church corrupts many good, sincere, and Godly people who are called to be leaders, turning many into a type of King Saul.

The mainstream of today's establishment Christianity parallels the time of Jesus and the Apostles, when the Lord came to call His sheep out of the apostate (fallen away) church of His day. It was a similar era of religious sectarianism and denominationalism under the umbrella of Judaism. The Babylonish harlot of 2,000 years ago is still among us, and she has taught and seduced many of God's servants, turning them into *"the merchants of Babylon."* God is now calling His people out of the modern Babylonish religious system so He can teach them, lead them, and bring them into unity outside the camp of the institutionalized corporate church.

You see, there are zero verses telling the Church to tithe, but many, many verses that speak about giving to those in need. And is giving to the building overhead or buying a $5,000 camera the same as giving to the poor? That is the difference between truth and leaven, what God said and what He never said. "*[A] little leaven* (author's note: law) *leaveneth the whole lump,*" said Paul to the Galatians.

Like the tithe, the New Testament knows nothing of the paid, salaried, professional clergy. The Lord sent His workers out saying, "*Freely ye have received, freely give.*" In Rev. 2:15 we read: "*So hast thou <u>also</u> some that hold the teaching of the Nicolaitans in like manner.*" Also in the church we find a human government hirarchy supported by tithes and salaries that rule the people. When Jesus said "<u>*beware*</u> *of the leaven of Herod*" He was speaking to the leaven of human government ruling in His kingdom! Nico-laitine means "overcome-the-laity" (people).

Some of you will fall on your face and repent because you now see the truth and are accountable. Others will repent for supporting an institutional temple, rather than God's temple—His people.

To those who still somehow disagree, or are afraid to disagree with your church leadership, we pray for you. We are not your enemies because we speak the truth in love.

To the rest, we say, "God bless you; may this book bring you liberty and the restored joy of true giving."

Author's Post Script

Messages In Dreams From The Lord

On the way home from a home group gathering, I was having doubts regarding leaving our mother church after so many years and if what we were doing was the right thing for us spiritually. In my mind, I told God we were willing to go back to the xyz church and humble ourselves if we were wrong in leaving. I did not want to be lost or cause anyone else to be lost. We had agonized over leaving the fellowship of our mother church after so much time. A dream was given from the Lord that night, December 9, 2004, and the Lord has graciously shown much of the meaning of the dream.

In this dream, I was riding as a front-seat passenger with two ministers dressed in black. The man driving was like two men blended into one: his features were like my first Pentecostal pastor and our last non-denominational pastor, somehow made into one man. I recognized both men's facial characteristics in the driver, and his voice was that of my last pastor.

We were traveling on a road that reminded me of Florida. This main road took us out of the developed area into a desert-like area that had fewer buildings. The black-suited driver and his minister friend in the back seat talked admiringly about Rev. P.M., a successful big-church-ministry pastor who had been well-paid to speak in our assembly a few years back. With relief, I was glad to leave the humidity and thought I could handle the dryness better and this was a better place to do something for the Lord. However, the road continued and changed into a dirt track road, narrower and bumpier. We slowed to negotiate a long, sharp bend, then ahead was a mountain. A short way up, the narrow track went over a knoll on the face of the mountain and the car stalled out. We backed down and said, "Take a run at it," but we failed again to climb the road. "Maybe if we got out and pushed," we said. Then the dream ended.

The interpretation: In the past, I had been assistant pastor and elder exercising prophetic and spiritual gifts (the front seat next to the driver). The black-suited ministers represent past and present leadership driving the Church in darkness.

We rode in a late eighties' model sedan, which represents the common corporate church model where I was saved in 1980. It had traditional meetings and formats, church programs and structure. We were driving through an uncomfortable, humid climate. Church had become very stifled with little fresh wind of the Holy Spirit to refresh us, though we longed for it.

The paved highway is the traditional, smooth and common-way church routine. Strong's defines *pavement* in Scripture as *a place of stumbling*. The desert-like area was a spiritual dry place we were driven to. Fewer buildings represent the end of the church-building paradigm. The road ahead to the future takes us to the wilderness and away from the past church environment.

The black-suited driver, and his minister friend in the back seat speaking admiringly about Rev. P.M., represents high-paid ministers, the model of big corporate church success, having men's reputation in admiration. The wilderness road is where the Church is going. The typical church, led by leaders in darkness (the black suit), will find the road slow and difficult. Then they will see the change of direction God has ordained and try to take people up the narrow way of the kingdom of God, but the old model corporate church will stall and falter backwards in spite of human effort pushing it. The institutional church as we know it cannot take up to Mount Zion, the Kingdom of the Lord.

In another dream given from the Lord, *I was driving a car through a downtown area. At a red light, I stopped behind a car with several young women riding in it.*

While stopped at the light, two women panhandlers walked up to the passenger side asking for money. The panhandlers were sort of aggressive and demanding and the passenger seat female became flustered as she fumbled to give one of the panhandlers some paper money. At one point, while she sorted through her cash, the panhandler saw a $10 bill and grabbed it. The passenger cried out for her to give it back and there was a brief scuffle, then the $10 bill was caught by a wind gust and before the passenger or the panhandler could grab it, the $10 bill was blown away.

The interpretation: The young women in the car are the church-goers, and the panhandlers are the churches that are continually asking for money, aggressively demanding funds. The $10 bill is the tithe that the panhandler church grabs. There is no Scriptural authority for the panhandler church to take the ten(th) as it has been *blown away* by the Holy Spirit in the New Testament!

About The Author

Rory O Moore was born in Modesto California on July 12, 1951 - a true Baby-Boomer. His father, Cecil, was a WWII US Navy veteran and his mother Helene, the oldest daughter of the Russell family who were literally tossed out of San Francisco in the quake of 1906. Raised in the small farming community of Los Banos, California, Rory was a child of the turbulent 60's, and grew up without Christianity. A typical 60's-70's sinner's lifestyle finally brought him to a place of surrender and a dramatic conversion to following Jesus Christ. Three years later he met and married his wife Linda and three wonderful children followed: Savanah, Jetrey, and Dustin.

He was a faithful member of several local churches beginning with a Baptist group, then thirteen years as a United Pentecostal (ordained and licensed), followed by eleven years as a founding member and elder of a local non-denominational church. He and Linda are currently members of the greater Body of Christ and fellowship with other believers in homes apart from the institutional church. God has graciously worked through their faith in bringing physical healing to many as the Lord continues to confirm His Word with signs and wonders.

Rory can be reached at: tttb@pacbell.net

Recommended Reading

Websites:

- Andrew Strom:
http://www.harvestnet.org/reports/nineliesfromStrom.htm
- David Eells:
http://www.americaslastdays.com Too much to list, HIGHLY recommended!
- "Secrets of the Early Church" online book by Andrew Strom:
http://homepages.ihug.co.nz/~revival/secrets-ch.html
- The church and the IRS: http://hushmoney.org/
http://www.guymalone.com/501c3church.htm
- Bible Numerics and the work of Ivan Panin
http://www.bereanpublishers.com/Apologetics/Book_Info_On_Ivan_Panin.htm

Books:

- Jaded: Hope for Believers Who Have Given Up on Church, but Not on God by Angela Kiesling
- Revolution by George Barna
- Pagan Christianity by Frank Viola
- Who is Your Covering? by Frank Viola
- The Present Future: Six Tough Questions for the Church -- by Reggie McNeal
- Sovereign God and Hidden Manna by David Eells